WE KILLED YAMAMOTO

The long-range P-38 assassination of the man behind Pearl Harbor, Bougainville 1943

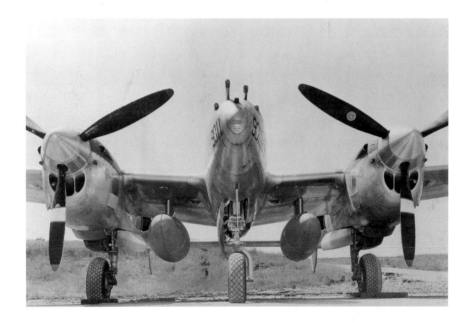

SI SHEPPARD

OSPREY PUBLISHING
Bloomsbury Publishing Plc
PO Box 883, Oxford, OX1 9PL, UK
1385 Broadway, 5th Floor, New York, NY 10018, USA
E-mail: info@ospreypublishing.com
www.ospreypublishing.com

OSPREY is a trademark of Osprey Publishing Ltd

First published in Great Britain in 2020

A catalog record for this book is available from the British Library.

ISBN: PB 9781472837868; eBook 9781472837875;
ePDF 9781472837844; XML 9781472837851

20 21 22 23 24   10 9 8 7 6 5 4 3 2 1

Battlescenes by Edouard A Groult
Cover art by Adam Tooby
Maps by www.bounford.com
3D BEVs by Alan Gilliland
Index by Fionbar Lyons
Typeset by PDQ Digital Media Solutions, Bungay, UK
Printed and bound in India by Replika Press Private Ltd.

Osprey Publishing supports the Woodland Trust, the UK's leading
woodland conservation charity.

To find out more about our authors and books visit
www.ospreypublishing.com. Here you will find extracts, author
interviews, details of forthcoming events and the option to sign up for our
newsletter.

ACKNOWLEDGEMENTS:

Special thanks to Bill Wolf and Matt Simek for their invaluable support.

DEDICATION:

Dedicated to the Fobbits, Pogues, and REMFs of the United States military:

That do contrive how many hands shall strike,
When fitness calls them on, and know by measure
Of their observant toil the enemies' weight…

William Shakespeare, *Troilus and Cressida*, Act I, Scene III

CONTENTS

INTRODUCTION

As within any corporate organization, there are hierarchics within the United States military. The special operations units – Delta Force, the Navy Seals, the Rangers – are the tip of the spear. Then there are the Marines, who look down on the Army, within which the Active Duty soldiers condescend to the National Guard. But everyone serving in the front lines despises the "Fobbits," "Pogues," and "REMFs" who serve behind desks and have never ventured into the field, never seen a shot fired in anger, never held a comrade in their arms as they bleed out.

While taking nothing from the sacrifices of the combat veterans, those who serve in support roles play a vital part in the collaborative effort necessary for fighting a successful war. Seldom has this been so with higher stakes to play for than during World War II. Allied intelligence agencies played a critical role in exposing the strategic frameworks and compromising the tactical initiatives of Nazi Germany and Imperial Japan. If one exemplar stands out from this conflict it is the US mission to intercept Japanese Admiral Isoroku Yamamoto in the South Pacific on April 18, 1943. This was the perfect marriage of intelligence breakthrough and operational initiative, the ideal partnership between men who never met – the codebreakers in basement offices far behind the lines, and the fighter pilots based in the malarial tropics far from home.

The development of US codebreaking

The origins of the US codebreaking services that were to play so significant a role in the Pacific during World War II can be traced back to Herbert O. Yardley, a civil service telegrapher in the State Department who proposed the establishment of a cipher bureau under the intelligence division after joining the Signal Corps of the Army during World War I. The idea was quickly adopted and an office was created under the title Military Intelligence Service (MIS). Yardley was put in charge and organized MIS into five subsections, which included encoding outgoing and deciphering incoming army messages. MIS was disbanded at the end of World War I, but one subsection, the Code and Cipher Solution office, was retained to crack the codes and ciphers of the country's enemies. Relocated to the State Department, it was the first organization of its kind to be permanently embedded within the US military establishment.

Japan had been a US ally during World War I, but the island nation had long been identified as a potential threat to US interests in the Pacific. It was for this reason that five agents of the Navy Department's Office of Naval Intelligence (ONI) broke into a Japanese consulate building and photographed Japan's top-secret naval codebook. This code was given the official designation of "JN-1" because it was the first Japanese navy code obtained by the US.

In December 1923 the Navy established a Research Desk within the Code and Signal Section of the Office of Naval Communications. Officially charged merely with safeguarding the security of American fleet codes, the unit was quietly given the task of penetrating the Japanese equivalents. A small staff of cryptographers was hired and the Navy thus established its own Cipher Bureau, colloquially dubbed the "Black Chamber." The first director of the Research Desk, Lieutenant Laurence F. Safford, persuaded his superiors to let him set up listening stations in key locations to intercept Japanese radio transmissions. As a result of his proposal, the first Pacific electronic monitoring station was set up on Guam. Additional monitoring stations were later established at Shanghai and in the Philippines.

Naval Communications was called OP-20 in the abbreviation system begun when Congress in 1915 approved creation of the Office of the Chief of Naval Operations; its communications security section carried the designation OP-20-G from 1926. That same year, Safford was succeeded by Lieutenant Joseph J. Rochefort. In collaboration with a team working under Agnes Meyer Driscoll at the Code and Signal Section of the Director of Naval Communications, and utilizing new business technology like frequency counters, card sorters, and key-punch machines, the Research Desk succeeded in breaking a succession of Japanese codes.

American cryptology suffered a setback when Herbert Hoover's Secretary of State, Henry L. Stimson, was briefed on the Black Chamber. He promptly ordered State Department funds be withdrawn from all of Yardley's activities. Disillusioned, bitter, and out of a job, Yardley contacted Japanese

Yamamoto doffs his cap in salute as he bids farewell to the pilot of a Zero fighter from the No. 204 Air Group during Operation *I-Go*, Rabaul, 1943. (Getty Images)

A Japanese radio transceiver, manufactured in June 1942. The Japanese designated this model as Type 94-6; the 6 is a model number, while the 94 specifies it was designed in the Japanese year 2594, or 1934. It was carried in a leather case with a shoulder strap and designed to be operated while walking, with voice or built-in Morse key. In the cat and mouse game of intelligence and counter-intelligence, communications experts in the Japanese mobile radio units, having identified the US frequencies, would come on the air to mimic American pilots, inserting false information. (Ralph Simpson, cipherhistory.com. CC BY-SA 4.0)

ambassador Tsuneo Matsudaira with an offer to sell the secrets he had so painstakingly accumulated for seven thousand dollars. The Japanese thus obtained all they needed to know of Yardley's codebreaking methods, his worksheets, and solutions to other codes, including those of Great Britain. In 1931 Yardley published a book entitled *The American Black Chamber* which revealed many of the codebreaking secrets he was privy to during his tenure in the business.

In the spring of 1929, the Army's Signal Intelligence Service (SIS) was created under William F. Friedman. In 1932, Friedman invented and patented a cryptographic system. Refinement of his prototype culminated in what became one of the most-used deciphering devices of World War II. He also invented a new machine which incorporated a message-authenticating system with a keyboard, the first to use an IBM card for cryptographic keying purposes.

Radio interception stations had been established at Guam (Station B) in March 1929 and at Shanghai (Station E) in 1935. A high-frequency direction-finding (HF/DF, or "huff-duff") station was installed at Cavite Navy Yard in the Philippines (Station C) in 1937. In the fall of 1941, Station C, by then including 41 radiomen, nine yeomen, and ten cryptanalytical personnel, moved to a new facility in Corregidor. At that time Hawaii (Station H, Hypo) had 69 radiomen. These outlying stations were complemented by others in the continental United States, including Alaska.

The number of radio operators had gradually increased. There were 55 in 1935, 70 in 1937, and 78 at the beginning of 1939. In early 1941 there was a total of 103 intercept operators, in addition to the network of direction-finding stations comprising eight stations with 85 operators and 116 radio receivers.

Intercept operators had to be able to copy 23 to 25 words a minute in Japanese. Once the students attained proficiency by hand, they were qualified to operate the RIP-5 machine, a typewriter modified to reproduce the Japanese Morse code letters in the *kana* (Japanese characters) they represented. Operators could record Japanese radio transmissions more easily, often faster than Imperial Japanese Navy (IJN) radiomen could draw the kana themselves.

OP-20-G's Lieutenant Jack Holtwick succeeded in devising a machine that could strip the ciphers off messages the Japanese sent using their first mechanism of this type, the so-called A Machine, known to the Americans as Red, and designed by IJN Captain Ito Jinsaburo. In 1939 the Japanese switched most of their diplomatic cable traffic to an even more complex new system, also designed by Ito Jinsaburo, which they called the B Machine, and which the Americans called Purple. Safford went to his Army counterpart, senior cryptanalyst William F. Friedman of the SIS within the Signal Corps. He assigned a team under Frank B. Rowlett, and work proceeded over a period of about 18 months. The SIS effort received support from the Army's chief signal officer, General Joseph O. Mauborgne, who liked to call the cryptanalysts his "magicians" and eventually called their product "Magic." The handful of people with security clearance for Magic were dubbed "Ultras." Neither the White House nor the State Department were given access. Since the Army lacked the necessary funds and resources to complete this mission, at Safford's initiative the Navy underwrote the cost while OP-20-G absorbed some routine SIS work to free Rowlett's team for the main task.

The first analog to the Purple machine (Type B Cipher Machine) reconstructed by the US Signals Intelligence Service. The unit contains 14 6x25 stepping switches. A hand-operated Red analog is also visible. (Mark Pellegrini at the US National Cryptologic Museum, Wikipedia. CC-BY-SA-2.5)

Operating in a group of about eight offices clustered around Rowlett's office in Room 3416 of the Munitions Building, the team succeeded in constructing an analog Purple machine. At OP-20-G, Lieutenant Francis A. Raven made a vital contribution by recognizing the method the Japanese used to compile the daily key used with the machine. Purple decrypts began to flow in September 1940, and soon, Washington was handling 50 to 75 Japanese messages a day in the Purple cipher.

The Japanese naval attaché code, which OP-20-G called Coral, was based on an encryption device introduced in September 1939 that used the same operating principles as the Purple diplomatic machines. US cryptanalysts had uncovered the basic features of Coral when they broke Purple, and further insight was gained when they solved the analogous Jade in 1943. Coral was first read by the Allies on March 13, 1944. Via the Japanese ambassador in Berlin, Coral turned out to be a prime intelligence source on German military operations.

In 1936, Lieutenant Thomas H. Dyer added a codebreaking capability to Station Hypo while stationed at Pearl Harbor. He was succeeded at the head of this operation by Lieutenant Commander Thomas B. Birtley, Jr., a former head of OP-20-G's translation section. Birtley and Lieutenant Ransom Fullinwider were at that time the only Japanese-language officers with the combat intelligence unit.

The Japanese revised their fleet code in mid-1939. This new alternative happened to be the 25th Japanese Navy code the Americans had tackled, so OP-20-G called it JN-25. A variant, JN-25(b), went into effect in December 1940. In response, now Commander Joseph J. Rochefort, who had been assigned to various roles on active duty with the Fleet, was notified in April 1941 that he would be transferred to head Hypo. The station was located in the basement of the administration building of the Commander-in-Chief of the Pacific Fleet (CINCPAC) headquarters at the submarine base at Pearl Harbor. Rochefort was in charge of a radio intelligence unit designated Fleet Radio Unit, Pacific (FRUPAC). In addition to deciphering enemy messages, Rochefort's unit kept track of all ship movements in the Pacific along with weather information and forecasts. His team included 29 intercept operators and perhaps 20 direction-finding specialists. One of his first actions was to change the organization's formal name to Combat Intelligence Unit (CIU). As it expanded the CIU moved to air-conditioned offices in the basement at the Diamond Head (southeast) end of the 14th Naval District headquarters building. By June the CIU had just under 80 persons involved in interception or direction finding and about 20 in its processing and codebreaking element. Rochefort transferred Hypo from a peacetime routine to an eight-day week in which his people would each work six days, then have two off. On September 4 the Navy increased enlisted billets provided for the CIU to 100 yeomen at Pearl Harbor plus 92 radiomen and two yeomen for intercept and other activities.

Infrastructure was still inadequate. Intercepts still had to be physically carried by bicycle, motorcycle, or jeep from the outstations down to the district office, rather than flashed by teletype. "This was just lousy," Rochefort observed. "It's like having a million-dollar organization with a ten-cent-store communication system."

Worse was the lack of coordination between different agencies. Admiral John Godfrey's July 1941 report on US intelligence concluded that

> cooperation between the various organisations is inadequate and sources are not coordinated to the mutual benefit of the departments concerned. There is little contact between the intelligence officers of the different departments ... The Office of Naval Intelligence is in danger of degenerating into a graveyard for statistics because it is inclined to regard intelligence as an end in itself.

Rochefort's team was not informed that US army codebreakers led by Frank Rowlett had cracked Japan's Purple diplomatic cipher in August 1940, nor about the ONI's acquisition of the Orange code from a Japanese freighter in San Francisco in May 1941, nor of the interception of a J-19 consular code communication from Tokyo to its Hawaii consulate on September 24, requesting the precise locations of US battleships inside Pearl Harbor.

The location of Japan's *Kido Butai* aircraft carrier battlegroup was lost in mid-November. On December 3, US intelligence operators were informed the Japanese had ordered all their diplomatic missions to destroy codes and ciphers. Four days later, all the intelligence team could do was watch helplessly as Japanese aircraft roamed at will in the skies over Pearl Harbor.

ORIGINS

Codebreaking from Pearl Harbor to Midway

The Japanese strike force was commanded by Chūichi Nagumo, but the architect of the Pearl Harbor operation was Isoroku Yamamoto, the Commander-in-Chief (C-in-C) of the Imperial Japanese Navy Combined Fleet. In his character, Yamamoto encapsulated a cosmopolitan worldview with fierce nationalist patriotism and a gambler's instincts. As a young officer he had served under Admiral Togo Heihachiro during the Russo-Japanese War, losing two fingers on his left hand during the battle of Tsushima. Study at Harvard University and two postings as a naval attaché in Washington, DC (where he learned to speak fluent English) gave him a broad understanding of America's industrial and military capacity. In the cut-throat world of Japanese politics during the 1930s, his outspoken opposition to the Army's agenda of adventurism in China and an alliance with Nazi Germany endangered his life. However, as his country drifted toward war with the United States, Yamamoto was duty-bound to optimize Japan's chances of emerging victorious from the conflict, regardless of his own deep reservations regarding the outcome. His approach was to make the opening move, hitting the enemy hard in a preliminary first strike, then keeping him off balance with a succession of offensive actions while pushing for a decisive battle. He foresaw the critical importance of airpower in achieving his goals. As early as 1915, Yamamoto was quoted as saying, "the most important ship of the future will be a ship to carry aeroplanes." Yamamoto would tell friends the battleship, the traditional embodiment of naval force projection, now amounted to nothing more than the "elaborate religious scrolls which old people hang up in their homes."

Even after Pearl Harbor, as Japan swept the United States and the European colonial powers from the western Pacific and so many others in the imperial military establishment allowed themselves to become swept up in the euphoria of the "victory disease," Admiral Isoroku Yamamoto never harbored any illusions about the nature of the trials to come. In a letter written to his nephew at the end of December 1941 he had noted, "The first stage of operations – i.e., the assaults on the Philippines, Hong Kong, Malaya, and the Dutch East Indies – will, I'm sure, prove no trouble; the real outcome will be determined after that, in the second stage." (Getty Images)

Kido Butai was his instrument in pursuit of his agenda; Pearl Harbor was the opening gambit in its realization.

The apparent success of the strike against Pearl Harbor made Yamamoto, its architect, public enemy number one in the US. By the same token, he emerged as the hero of Japan; if the Emperor embodied the nation, it was Yamamoto who personified the military and the war effort.

As the Japanese offensive unfolded, the Allied position in the Pacific collapsed. Centuries-old empires folded in weeks, as the Dutch possessions in the Indies were engulfed and the British, evicted from Hong Kong, Singapore, Malaya, and Burma, fell back to India and Australia. The US could do nothing to save its garrisons in the Philippines. The sole proactive step taken by the US Navy during this period was to cull the dead wood from command posts and introduce new, and more aggressive, leadership. Ernest J. King was appointed C-in-C of the US Fleet. Chester W. Nimitz was appointed C-in-C of the US Pacific Fleet. And William F. ("Bull") Halsey was assigned command of US naval forces in the South Pacific. This triumvirate – King in Washington, Nimitz at Pearl Harbor, and Halsey in the South Pacific – would take the fight to the Japanese with authority and increasing potency.

That was in the future. Meanwhile, the inexorable Japanese expansion in the six months following Pearl Harbor had severely compromised the Allied intelligence-gathering apparatus by engulfing its operating sites. Station E was long abandoned; Station B fell with Guam. Station C personnel, along with their direction-finding gear, kana typewriters, and the top-secret Red and Purple machines, were evacuated to Melbourne, Australia, in a series of increasingly harrowing submarine missions between February and April 1942, just ahead of the Japanese occupation of the Philippines.

With the intelligence agencies of the disparate anti-Japanese alliance so badly disrupted and dispersed, a conference held in April 1942 established the Allied Intelligence Bureau (AIB), formed as an arm of General Douglas MacArthur's Southwest Pacific (SOWESPAC) General Headquarters, to coordinate the gathering and sharing of information. One critical source of intelligence was the informal network of observers established in New Guinea and the Solomon Islands by Australian naval reservist Eric A. Feldt. Dubbed Ferdinand (its name whimsically taken from the children's story *Ferdinand the Bull*) these coastwatchers, composed of military personnel, civilian expats, and their native allies, monitored Japanese units and radioed in their movements to Allied HQs throughout the region.

The AIB was also responsible for liaison with guerrilla fighters in the Philippines and elsewhere, including special commando operations (such as one mission in Singapore harbor in late 1943 that sank six cargo ships totaling 46,000 tons). By the end of the war, the AIB was officially credited with carrying out 264 missions, during which 164 men lost their lives and another 178 went missing.

SOWESPAC also created an Allied Translator and Interpreter Section, which specialized in reporting on captured Japanese documents, and served as the locus for another intelligence fusion center, the Seventh

Fleet Intelligence Center (SEFIC). The Australian government's codebreaking unit, the Central Bureau, and the Belconnen-based Fleet Radio Unit Melbourne (FRUMEL) also contributed to the ever-expanding intelligence network.

Station Hypo at Pearl Harbor remained the center of the Allied intelligence web. Rochefort made a critical breakthrough when he detected a pattern in which the decoded Japanese words *koryaku butai* (strike force) were followed by two letters, the first of which designated a zone in the Pacific, the second a location within that zone – for example, MM represented the Philippine zone and the capital city, Manilla. All two-letter codes beginning with A were in the American-controlled zone. Rochefort sensed great significance in a partial decrypt containing the phrase *koryaku butai* AF.

On April 7, OP-20-G informed Admiral King that a new extension of Japanese air search patterns clearly indicated interest in the Coral Sea. On April 8, Rochefort correctly predicted the Japanese were moving on Port Moresby in Papua New Guinea, having identified RZP as its code designation. On April 17, coincident with the solidifying intelligence picture, King gave Nimitz command of the Coral Sea area.

By early May, Hypo was receiving between 500 and 1,000 intercepts per day, about 60 percent of all Japanese transmissions, of which it was able to read fragments of some 40 percent. On May 5 and 6 there were repeated messages from Admiral Kajioka's Port Moresby Occupation Force giving his position and plans for sailing south on May 7. That's where American search planes found him, initiating the sequence of air strikes that became the main action in the battle of the Coral Sea.

On May 9, Rochefort was able to inform Nimitz the Japanese fleet would sail for a major operation on the 21st, but he could not confirm the target destination. However, a Central Pacific focus was confirmed by the decrypt of Second Fleet Operations Order Number 22 on May 11, which directed concentration of an occupation force for the forthcoming campaign at Saipan. Two days later the code designator MI was used in connection with the occupation force.

FRUMEL's first key contribution was a decrypt showing that the Japanese had abandoned the plan for amphibious landing at Port Moresby in favor of an offensive across the Owen Stanley Mountains. This made the presence of American carriers in the South Pacific superfluous and enabled Nimitz to justify recalling them.

Another FRUMEL coup was decryption of a First Air Fleet order signaling Nagumo's intention to leave his training bases and marshal forces for the operation. Traffic analysis identified the ships in the Japanese order of battle. By monitoring the Japanese buildup, FRUMEL established the operation would be against either Midway Island or Hawaii.

The immediate response of then Vice Admiral William "Bull" Halsey when he arrived at Pearl Harbor on December 8, 1941, was to pledge, "Before we're through with them, the Japanese language will be spoken only in Hell." Serving as commander, Carrier Division 2, aboard his flagship the USS *Enterprise*, Halsey took the fight to the Japanese, most significantly in commanding the April 18, 1942, Doolittle raid on Tokyo. In this capacity he came to know and respect "Pete" Mitscher, whom he subsequently appointed Commander Air, Solomon Islands (COMAIRSOLS) on Guadalcanal. In his judgment, "I knew we'd probably catch hell from the Japs in the air. That's why I sent Pete Mitscher up there. Pete was a fighting fool and I knew it." (NARA)

The gist of Nagumo's carrier operations plan was revealed in a May 16 message reporting his intention to stage air attacks beginning two days before the invasion and starting from a point 50 miles northwest of MI. FRUMEL's intelligence confirmed Rochefort's at Pearl Harbor. That satisfied King, who cabled Nimitz on May 17 his full agreement with the latter's belief that the Japanese were about to attack Midway, overriding OP-20-G's concern that Alaska was the primary target.

On May 13, a Japanese message had been intercepted instructing the supply ship *Goshu Maru* to load stores at Saipan and then proceed to AF. To confirm the designation, on May 19, one of Rochefort's team, Jasper Holmes, suggested the naval air station on Midway be sent a ciphered message by undersea cable instructing its operators to send an uncoded wireless signal to Pearl reporting problems with its freshwater evaporator and requesting supplies of fresh water. This message was duly intercepted by the IJN special duty group on Wake, which sent out an immediate report of the water problem on AF. Tokyo quickly informed fleet units that MI was short of fresh water. This dispatch was intercepted and broken by FRUMEL. For added confirmation, the US intercepted a Combined Fleet message listing new geographic designators that were to be used temporarily; AF was listed as MI.

The following day, another member of Rochefort's team, Red Lasswell, broke the Japanese order for the assault. On May 27, two more team members, Joe Finnegan and Ham Wright, broke a signal identifying the dates of the strikes – June 3 against the Aleutians, June 4 against Midway. Nimitz made the pivotal decision to commit all three of his carriers against the enemy at Midway.

On the morning of May 27 Rochefort was summoned to headquarters to give a briefing on Japanese intentions. He arrived a half-hour late, having waited to get the final results from the translation. This was the last data there was going to be, for at midnight May 25 the Japanese had implemented their long-delayed code change, superseding JN-25(b) with JN-25(c) and denying the Allies further communications intelligence until the new code could be broken.

Rochefort described the general features of the MI plan, including Yamamoto's disposition of forces, which would include the four aircraft carriers of *Kido Butai*, the *Akagi*, *Kaga*, *Hiryu*, and *Soryu*. When Nimitz demanded specifics, his intelligence officer, Lieutenant Commander Edwin T. Layton, concluded: "They will come in from the northwest on bearing 325 degrees and they will be sighted at about 175 miles from Midway, and the time will be about [0600] Midway time."

Rarely can one side have entered battle so entirely aware of the enemy's strength and intentions. When the initial sighting reports of the Japanese fleet arrived at CINCPAC headquarters, Nimitz went to his operations plot room to fix the location on the maps. Once this was established, he immediately turned to Layton. "Well," Nimitz said, "you were only five miles, five degrees, and five minutes off." Forewarned is forearmed; the battle of Midway was a triumph for the US Navy and a disaster for the IJN,

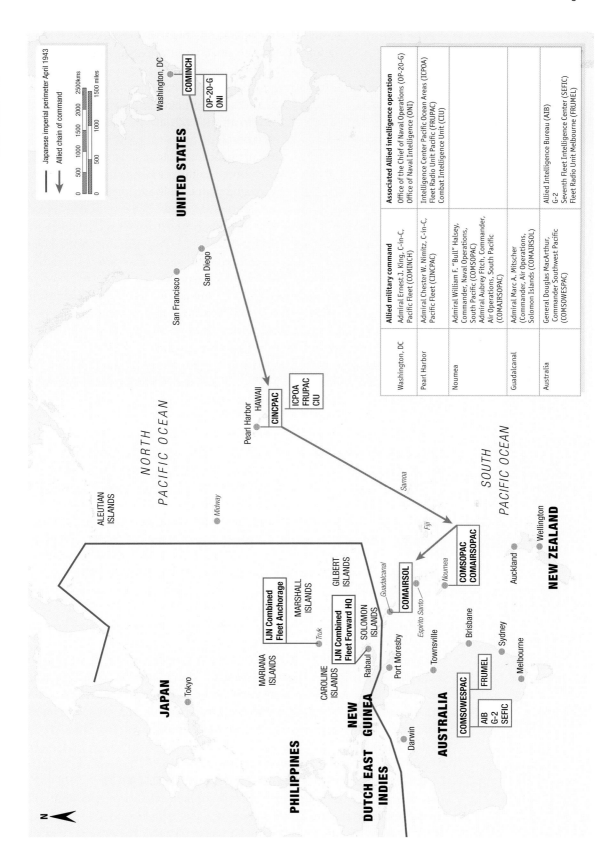

	Allied military command	Associated Allied intelligence operation
Washington, DC	Admiral Ernest J. King, C-in-C, Pacific Fleet (COMINCH)	Office of the Chief of Naval Operations (OP-20-G) Office of Naval Intelligence (ONI)
Pearl Harbor	Admiral Chester W. Nimitz, C-in-C, Pacific Fleet (CINCPAC)	Intelligence Center Pacific Ocean Areas (ICPOA) Fleet Radio Unit Pacific (FRUPAC) Combat Intelligence Unit (CIU)
Noumea	Admiral William F. "Bull" Halsey, Commander, Naval Operations, South Pacific (COMSOPAC) Admiral Aubrey Fitch, Commander, Air Operations, South Pacific (COMAIRSOPAC)	
Guadalcanal	Admiral Marc A. Mitscher (Commander, Air Operations, Solomon Islands (COMAIRSOL)	
Australia	General Douglas MacArthur, Commander Southwest Pacific (COMSOWESPAC)	Allied Intelligence Bureau (AIB) G-2 Seventh Fleet Intelligence Center (SEFIC) Fleet Radio Unit Melbourne (FRUMEL)

Japanese imperial perimeter April 1943

Allied chain of command

0   500   1000   1500   2000   2500kms
0   500   1000   1500 miles

UNITED STATES

Washington, DC

COMINCH

OP-20-G
ONI

San Francisco

San Diego

NORTH
PACIFIC OCEAN

Pearl Harbor   HAWAII

CINCPAC

ICPOA
FRUPAC
CIU

Midway

Samoa

Fiji

SOUTH
PACIFIC OCEAN

COMSOPAC
COMAIRSOPAC

Noumea

COMAIRSOL

Guadalcanal

Espírito Santo

Wellington

Auckland

NEW ZEALAND

ALEUTIAN
ISLANDS

JAPAN

Tokyo

MARIANA
ISLANDS

CAROLINE
ISLANDS

Truk

IJN Combined
Fleet Anchorage

MARSHALL
ISLANDS

GILBERT
ISLANDS

SOLOMON
ISLANDS

IJN Combined
Fleet Forward HQ

Rabaul

NEW
GUINEA

Port Moresby

Townsville

Brisbane

Sydney

Melbourne

FRUMEL

COMSOWESPAC

AIB
G-2
SEFIC

AUSTRALIA

Darwin

DUTCH EAST
INDIES

PHILIPPINES

N

3TH AFPL 2-4 15:00 AG 96
RAINWATER IN E.M AREA

Its location in the South Pacific notwithstanding, Guadalcanal was no tropical paradise. When they seized the island on August 7, 1942, the 10,900 US personnel on Guadalcanal had food for just two weeks, ammunition for less than one. The Marines were on half rations until mid-September, and even that was only made possible by utilizing provisions liberated from the Japanese. When those were gone, US personnel subsisted on dehydrated potatoes and SPAM or cold hash. Some enterprising individuals resorted to exploding grenades in the Lunga River to catch fish. The tents, bedding, and blankets, too, were all captured from the Japanese. In this environment, almost everyone contracted dysentery and/or malaria. The climate was as changeable as it could be unsparing, as illustrated in this photo of the enlisted men's area in the wake of one of Guadalcanal's periodic torrential downpours. (NARA)

which lost all four of its carriers in exchange for just one American flattop, the *Yorktown*.

Having definitively proved its mettle, the radio intelligence unit at Pearl Harbor continued to grow in conjunction with deepening hostilities. By late May 1942, Station Hypo consisted of two cryptanalysts, three traffic analysts, nine language officers, 30 cryptographic clerks or assistants on that or traffic analysis, 56 kana intercept operators, and a clerical force of 70 persons. By August, this had increased to 33 cryptanalysts or traffic experts, 21 language officers, 92 kana operators (with 46 more in training), and 137 yeomen or specialists. Orders were issued to expand the number of operators to 500, including 17 more cryptanalysts or traffic people, 24 language officers, and 27 kana operators, plus specialists.

Along with expansion came reorganization. In July some 17 officers and 59 men were ordered to Pearl Harbor to create the Intelligence Center Pacific Ocean Areas (ICPOA). The first officers to report were given desks among the Combat Intelligence Unit at Fleet Radio Unit, Pacific (FRUPAC), the name assigned Hypo in the new intelligence hierarchy. In the event, this would have no place for Rochefort. Nimitz had paid him the tribute he was due: "This officer deserves a major share of the credit for the victory at Midway." But these words were to be Rochefort's only reward. The victim of interagency rivalry, his recommendation for the Distinguished Service Medal was denied, and on October 14 he was relieved of his post and assigned to command a floating dry dock in San Francisco.

The Japanese military could not have eliminated Rochefort any more efficiently or ruthlessly than its US counterpart had, but, even in his absence, the people and programs he had put in place continued to score successes. The Japanese code for weather data transmission became 85 percent transparent on September 29, when Station Hypo got access to captured codebooks. On October 1, the substitution table for the code activated that very day was recovered, with the first code groups broken two days later.

By October 15, Pearl Harbor had established the call signs and radio frequencies used by two Japanese aircraft carriers, giving a position that differed by just one degree of longitude and one of latitude from the location given in a US aircraft sighting report the same day. By that date, the focus of the war had shifted, and Allied forces in the embattled sector would need all the help they could get.

Intelligence in the battle for Guadalcanal

The two sides drew apart after Midway, the Japanese wounded but still dangerous, the Americans buoyed but – for the moment – unable to follow up. The focus shifted south to the Solomon Islands. The ensuing war of attrition on and around Guadalcanal would prove the decisive campaign in the Pacific, in large part due to the contributions of Allied intelligence.

On January 29, 1942, the IJN authorized Directive No. 47, providing for control of the waters north and east of Australia by means of taking over key areas in New Guinea and the Solomon Islands, including Lae, Salamaua, and Tulagi. In his grand strategic vision, Yamamoto had argued "naval operations of the future will consist of capturing an island, then building an airfield in as short a time as possible – within a week or so – moving up air units and using them to gain air and surface control over the next stretch of ocean." But it would be the Americans who used this doctrine against him. On August 7, the Marines seized the Japanese-held island of Guadalcanal, including its unfinished airstrip. This would become Henderson Field, base for what would be dubbed the Cactus Air Force. Stung, the Japanese committed additional naval, air, and land forces to reclaim the island. The Americans responded in kind and both sides, stretched to their limits, found themselves entangled in a brutal fight neither could back away from.

The Japanese were determined to regain the initiative in the Solomons, and the Americans knew they were coming. On August 17 the Combined Fleet implemented its call sign change, always a suggestion of impending operations. SOPAC (South Pacific Area Command) issued an intelligence summary that day announcing the carriers of *Kido Butai* were definitely heading south, if they had not already set out.

The ensuing carrier battle of the Eastern Solomons on August 24, 1942 was inconclusive, but was enough to convince the Japanese their convoys of merchant ships were too vulnerable to US airpower. As an alternative, the Japanese elected to resupply their forces on Guadalcanal by resorting to night runs via destroyers or submarines. Dubbed the Tokyo Express by the Americans, these runs were far from sufficient to meet the logistical demands of the Japanese, who were attempting to build up their forces on land in order to drive the Marines back into the ocean. Japanese troops, who suffered appalling deprivation, dubbed Guadalcanal "Starvation Island."

In order to suppress American airpower, the Japanese Naval Air Force (JNAF) initiated an interdiction campaign in late August that continued unabated for four months, with almost daily raids on Henderson, usually conducted by two to three squadrons (20 to 30 bombers) covered by roughly equal numbers of fighters.

As the Japanese increased their daily effort against Guadalcanal, the Cactus Air Force found itself hard pressed to respond, even though the Americans could rely on observation of enemy action from the coastwatcher network and the advantage of operating over

Its superiority in the air counted for little when a Lightning was caught on the ground. There is little left of this P-38 beyond its engines, wingtips, and nose. At the height of the struggle for Guadalcanal, shelling from Japanese warships cruising offshore reduced the fighting strength of the Cactus Airforce to just a handful of operational aircraft. Even after the US wrested back control of the sea lanes, Japanese bombing raids – the so-called "Tojo Time" – continued to take their toll. (NARA)

Burning aircraft and, in the center at a distance, a burning hangar on Henderson Field, Guadalcanal, in the aftermath of a Japanese bombing raid. Captain John W. Mitchell, who had arrived just a week earlier as flight leader of twelve P-39s, never forgot his experience of the Japanese shelling of Henderson Field on October 14: 'We all made a dive for our foxholes and then all hell broke loose. There were 15 of us crammed into a foxhole built for about 8 men. It was hot and you couldn't move without kicking someone in the face. Star shell and shells with horribly beautiful green and white flares were exploding over our heads. Coconut palms were gashed and completely knocked down… For three hours this went on and then suddenly ceased. We gradually emerged but we stuck close to the fox hole that night and there was no sleep.' (Getty Images)

their own base. Unlike carrier combat air controllers, who vectored fighters to their prey, the Marines were forced to resort to "vertical interception" because base radio, which worked poorly amid tropical humidity, could hardly be heard more than about 20 miles away. When to order fighters into the air became a daily dilemma of huge importance: too soon, and the planes used up their gas and had to land, leaving them sitting ducks for attack; too late and the interceptors would be unable to gain enough altitude to attain favorable positions. Radio intelligence made the difference because the JNAF would use the same frequencies and set up a small net for their formation right after takeoff from Rabaul. All the radiomen had to do was listen for Japanese on the bomber frequencies and notify Cactus ground control, which usually gave advance warning of any incoming strike at least 15 minutes before it showed up on radar.

Navy radiomen on Guadalcanal also brought in the first Japanese radio sets captured during the war, a boon for American technical intelligence. The unit monitored the general broadcast circuit from Rabaul, contributed to direction finding for sea and air transmissions, and helped the Marines identify Japanese Army units on Guadalcanal itself.

On September 3, Brigadier General Roy Geiger, commander of the 1st Marine Air Wing, arrived to establish a forward air command post. A radio intelligence element arrived in mid-September with the convoy that brought the 7th Marine Regiment. This was a tiny two-man direction-finding unit that helped generate target information for the Cactus Air Force. A couple of weeks later they were augmented by a full mobile radio detachment led by Lieutenant Commander Daniel J. McCallum. This unit, soon dubbed the "Cactus Crystal Ball," based itself in a tunnel dug into a hillock below Henderson Field. Among its most important contributions was a daily list of radio fixes on Japanese ships, used to target air strikes.

Summarizing the submissions of its disparate intelligence assets, on October 6 CINCPAC noted the expanding Japanese Army and elite Special Naval Landing Forces (SNLF) presence in the Solomons and predicted an impending attempt to overcome the Marines. Two days later, CINCPAC confirmed the Tokyo Express was running at full capacity, pointed out the steady flow of aircraft to Rabaul, located the Sendai Division's Chief of Staff on Guadalcanal, and commented that the Japanese 17th Army was "increasingly associated" with the island. On October 10, CINCPAC mentioned the Nagumo and Kondo forces in relation to the Solomons, again associated the

17th Army with Cactus, located the Sendai Division as possibly on the island with the Kawaguchi Brigade, listed several SNLF units present in the islands, and ominously led with: "The impression is gained that the enemy may be getting ready for larger-scale operations in the Guadalcanal area."

This wasn't long in coming. Just after midnight on October 14, Japanese battleships hammered Henderson Field with 973 14in. shells. Sunrise revealed a scene of utter devastation. Only seven SBD dive-bombers and 35 fighters could still fly. The Pagoda was demolished. Enough aviation fuel survived for just one mission. Mechanics worked desperately on crippled planes. On the night of October 15, Japanese cruisers lashed Henderson with 752 8in. shells; the night after that, they landed an additional 926, inflicting more damage on aircraft and gouging out more of the craters that now pockmarked the runways.

This dramatic photo captures the moment a Japanese air raid over Guadalcanal has caught a US troop transport ship in the act of disgorging its complement of reinforcements into landing boats. The three Japanese aircraft circled are passing over Henderson Field. Incidents with life-or-death consequences like this were a routine feature of life on Guadalcanal. (NARA)

At dawn on the fifteenth, Marines were outraged to see Japanese transport ships unloading in broad daylight across the Sound. The Cactus Air Force struggled to respond. Fuel barrels that had been cached in swamps and groves were located and laboriously hauled to the strips, while frantic appeals were made to SOPAC to bring in gasoline aboard its daily flights and even via submarine. Mechanics rushed repairs. Ten SBD dive-bombers and seven Army fighter-bombers were able to take off and hit the transports at Tassafaronga Point, destroying three and forcing the others to withdraw.

That day, codebreakers reported that the pattern of radio traffic showed Yamamoto had taken direct command of operations. The following day, intelligence confirmed the traffic flow from the Combined Fleet and reported that the Japanese appeared to have focused all their attention on the Solomons. The CINCPAC war diary for October 17 read, "It now appears that we are unable to control the sea" in the Guadalcanal area. Resupply of the American garrison could be accomplished only "at great expense."

Starting on October 19, US intelligence tabulated a reduction in high-level, high-priority message volume, ominously suggesting Yamamoto's offensive was underway. The next day it furnished a new location for *Kido Butai* and associated carrier commander Nagumo with surface fleet Vice Admiral Kondo.

This was the prelude to the desperate fighting for the perimeter of Henderson Field that commenced on the night of 24 October. While the Marines dug in, Roy Geiger told his airmen they would fly to the last, then join ground units. Lieutenant Harold Larsen, whose Torpedo-8 had no

A P-38 of 339th FS, parked adjacent to the coconut plantation that formed one boundary of Fighter Two airstrip. There is another P-38 and a Marine SBD tucked into a revetment in the background. Note the elevated surface; the runway is composed of Marston Matting – perforated aluminum plates – which helped solve the mud problem created by the incessant rain on Guadalcanal. The Seabees pre-loaded dump trucks with earth to fill a typical crater, and precut Marston matting to replace runway panels, discovering they could fix the damage from a Japanese 550-pound bomb in about forty minutes. (Matt Simek)

TBF Avengers left, took his pilots and ground crews out to Bloody Ridge to fight as infantry.

After savage fighting, the Japanese were repulsed, but it had been a near-run thing. By October 26, even with ground crews working frantically to cannibalize wrecked aircraft, Geiger had barely been able to muster a dozen Marine F4Fs, 11 Navy and Marine SBDs, three P-400s, three P-39s, and one F4F-7 photo-reconnaissance plane.

Still, the Japanese would not concede. As they built up for another combined land and sea offensive, US intelligence monitored their progress. Codebreakers, already aware of convoys bringing Japanese 38th Division troops from Palau up to Rabaul, penetrated the dispatch containing Yamamoto's "Z-Day" operations order, sent in a JN-25 code transmission on November 8. The following day, CINCPAC predicted an "all out attempt upon Guadalcanal soon, using transports to carry Army troops and supported by carriers." Nimitz authorized a dispatch warning:

INDICATIONS THAT MAJOR OPERATION ASSISTED BY CARRIER STRIKING FORCE SLATED TO SUPPORT MOVEMENT ARMY TRANSPORTS TO GUADALCANAL …
WHILE THIS LOOKS LIKE A BIG PUNCH I AM CONFIDENT THAT YOU WITH YOUR FORCES WILL TAKE THEIR MEASURE

Coastwatcher reports confirmed the massing of Japanese naval strength. Radio fixes definitely put Admiral Kondo in the Solomons, and on November 14 he was reported to be in command. That same day, aircraft from Henderson Field and the *Enterprise* sank seven inbound transport ships. After US naval forces drove off the escorting warships that night, the four surviving Japanese transports beached near Tassafaronga in a desperate bid to deliver their cargoes. At first light, US aircraft and artillery found them and destroyed them.

It was the turning point of the campaign. At SOPAC, clutching the latest situation report, Halsey exulted to his staff, "We've got the bastards licked!" The Navy's brass hats had no hesitation in attributing the margin of difference to the intelligence assets under their command. At Pearl Harbor, Nimitz issued a commendation, perforce sent over the classified in-house Copek circuit:

ONCE AGAIN RADIO INTELLIGENCE HAS ENABLED THE FIGHTING FORCE OF THE PACIFIC AND SOUTHWEST PACIFIC TO KNOW WHERE AND WHEN TO HIT THE ENEMY

MY ONLY REGRET IS THAT OUR APPRECIATION, WHICH IS UNLIMITED,
CAN ONLY BE EXTENDED TO THOSE WHO READ THIS SYSTEM

From COMINCH in Washington, Admiral King added, "Well Done."

As the Japanese impetus waned, US forces continued to follow up on the inside information they were being fed by an ever-expanding network of sources. Allied intelligence identified Japanese construction of an airfield on Munda, enabling its interdiction; provided advance warning of Japanese destroyer sorties; and confirmed by name the arrival of Japanese reinforcements, including antiaircraft units, an infantry battalion, an artillery battery, and engineers.

Ironically, the only thing Allied intelligence missed was the fact that the Japanese had decided to cut their losses and withdraw from Guadalcanal at the end of 1942. They were gone by February 7 of the following year. At 1625hrs on February 9, US Marines and GIs under Major General Alexander Patch confirmed clearing Cactus. He messaged Halsey:

"TOKYO EXPRESS" NO LONGER HAS TERMINUS ON GUADALCANAL

At the close of the campaign, the Allies scored a minor victory that would have a huge impact in terms of the intelligence picture. This was the loss of the submarine *I-1* off Kamimbo Bay on January 29. Under Lieutenant Commander Sakamoto Eichi, the *I-1* was on a *mogura* (mole) submarine supply run to Guadalcanal with 60 soldiers on board. A series of late-January Ultra decrypts had mentioned I-boat cruises to Cactus, and the *I-1* was identified in the traffic. Several radio direction-finding stations in New Zealand tracked I-boat transmissions showing submarines nearing Guadalcanal. Based on this, Cactus naval command alerted all units to the presence of a Japanese submarine off Kamimbo. On the night of January 29, the New Zealand corvettes *Moa* and *Kiwi* detected the *I-1*. Lieutenant Commander Gordon Bridson's *Kiwi* dropped depth charges, forcing the *I-1* to the surface. Sakamoto ran for the coastline in a bid to beach the submarine. Because the vessels were so close together (less than 150 yards), Bridson gave orders to ram. When engine-room crew questioned the order the skipper insisted, then quipped that the action might be good for leave time – at first a weekend in Auckland then, as the battle continued, a full week, even a fortnight. *Kiwi*'s 4in. gun, illuminated by star shells from *Moa*, swept the deck of the *I-1*, wiped out Sakamoto's primary gun crew, and mortally wounded the commander himself. Bridson then rammed the *I-1* three times. The submarine finally ran aground on a reef 300 yards from the Guadalcanal shore.

The Allies were able to recover seven codebooks, including two in the JN-25 code, which provided lists of the Imperial Navy's geographic designators, radio call signs, short-time and area codes, and a wealth of technical data on Japanese submarines. The Imperial Navy immediately declared a cryptologic emergency, changed the additive tables used with JN-25, and began compiling a new codebook with different values. But

The Lightning made its debut as an interceptor at Guadalcanal on November 12, 1942, when eight P-38s were flown in by pilots of the newly formed 339th FS, 47th Fighter Group (FG). The next day another eight P-38s, assigned to the 39th FS, 35th FG, flew in from Port Moresby, New Guinea, on loan from the Fifth Air Force. In mid-January 1943 all USAAF units on Guadalcanal were subsumed into the Thirteenth Air Force. P-38s of the 339th scored the type's first kills in the South Pacific while escorting B-17 and B-24 bombers on a mission against Buin on November 18. Qualified pilots began transferring to the new fighter; Captain John W. Mitchell, who had three kills to his name flying the P-39, scored his first kill in a P-38 on January 5, 1943. He scored two more on January 27, making him the Thirteenth Air Force's first ace. (Matt Simek)

they did not change the basic codebook. "It was very useful to have a complete code, fleet vocabulary," Tom Dyer recalled: "It settled a number of arguments as to what word was used." Thanks to the *I-1* windfall, Allied codebreakers would stay two steps ahead on JN-25 for the duration of the war.

The Allied intelligence apparatus was both expanding and professionalizing even as the land campaign on Guadalcanal wound down. New technological innovations included the increasing use of punch cards and mechanical sorting devices, important in enabling cross-referencing information and thereby accelerating the pace of decryption, and the development of radio fingerprinting of individual Japanese operators, which helped identify the key enemy messages and could reveal the character of a given ship or unit or even its identity when call signs were not available.

At the time of Midway there had been 168 persons, including radio operators, in the Station Hypo codebreaking unit, with just two cryptanalysts and three traffic analysis experts. During the Eastern Solomons campaign FRUPAC had grown to 283 people, among them 54 experts in the code or traffic work or in the Japanese language, plus 46 additional radio intercept operators in training. The Navy ordered FRUPAC personnel increased to 500, with 17 more code experts and 24 extra language officers. Having outgrown its quarters, in early 1943 FRUPAC moved to a huge new wood-frame building near CINCPAC headquarters on Makalapa Hill, which it shared with the new ICPOA. By the end of the war FRUPAC had taken over the entire building, and an identical one had been built next door for ICPOA. By then the US Navy alone was operating 775 receivers across the Pacific entirely devoted to intercepting Japanese message traffic.

P-38s join the Cactus Air Force

Meanwhile, the fight continued on the front lines. A new dimension to the air war opened when the first P-38s arrived at Guadalcanal on November 12. First impressions were not positive. Because the P-38s had superior altitude performance, they were always assigned high cover, leading to other pilots dubbing the Lightning a "high altitude foxhole." In addition, existing tactical doctrine was not compatible with this unique new airframe. An after-action report dated November 18 bluntly stated, "the P-38 is not an escort fighter, as the plane is too unmaneuverable and blind." To compensate

for its vulnerabilities, and play to its strengths, a new tactical formation was introduced, with flights of four P-38s dispersed in echelon. Each flight leader had a wingman on his port, supported by an element leader and his wingman to starboard. Instead of mixing it up dogfighting with the more nimble Zero, the P-38s would dive from high altitude in attacking passes, then power away to regain the height advantage and repeat the process. As pilots came to appreciate the advantages of their mounts – which boasted the highest altitude, longest range, most powerful armament, and most rugged airframe of

any American fighter in theater – they in turn became more confident and aggressive, to the point where "it was a total turn-around," Marine Major John P. Condon noted; squadrons outfitted with P-38s were "the best airplanes and the best pilots we had."

Captain John Mitchell took over as 339th Fighter Squadron CO on November 25 and started to get results. On December 10, eight P-38s escorted 11 B-17s in an attack on Japanese ships in Buin Harbor. The P-38 pilots were credited with five Zeros destroyed, including one each for Lieutenant Doug Canning and his wingman, Lieutenant Delton Goerke. The same day, nine SBDs, nine P-39s, four P-38s, and four F4F Wildcats had engaged 14 Zeros during a raid on Munda, the US pilots reportedly downing five Japanese fighters, one of them being claimed by P-38 pilot Lieutenant Tom Lanphier.

When the 13th Air Force was formed in January 1943 it included two fighter groups, the 18th and 347th, with five P-39 squadrons, two P-40 squadrons, and the P-38-equipped 339th. By this time, with the Japanese threat having eased, and with the logistics chains improving day by day, the American presence on Guadalcanal was both expanding and becoming more specialized. Henderson Field was now used by the transports and bombers; two new airfields had been constructed for the interceptors. Fighter One, southeast of Henderson, was used by the Marine fighters; Fighter Two, northwest of Henderson, was shared by the Marine and Army Air Force fighters. The P-38s were at Fighter Two, with the P-39s, P-40s, F4Fs, and F-4U-1 Corsairs.

On January 5, Mitchell himself scored his first kill in a P-38 (he had claimed three victories in P-39s the previous year). Mitchell claimed his fifth and sixth victories on January 27, making him the 13th Air Force's first ace. Two days later, Mitchell received permission to try a night interception when a formation of Betty bombers raided Guadalcanal after midnight. The entire island watched the spectacle as the bomber, ablaze in the darkness, crashed to earth for his seventh victory.

Captain John W. Mitchell arrived at Guadalcanal on October 7, 1942, leading a flight of 12 P-39s. He quickly found himself in the thick of combat as the struggle for the island reached its climax. In his account of an October 22 attack run against Japanese transport ships, he stated, "The antiaircraft we had experienced was nothing compared to what we encountered that morning. All the escorting warships and transports seemed to be a single sheet of flame and shrapnel was falling so fast that the water looked as though there was a heavy rain squall going on." Mitchell's qualities as a pilot and a leader commanded almost immediate recognition. The following month, already credited with three kills, he was promoted to Major and Commanding Officer of the 339th FS. (Matt Simek)

A panorama of Fighter Two airstrip, Guadalcanal. By April 1943, Henderson Field was reserved exclusively for bomber operations (light bombers for missions ranging out to New Georgia, heavy bombers that could reach all the way to Bougainville). F4F Wildcats and F4U Corsairs were stationed at Fighter One, while P-38 Lightnings, P-40 Warhawks, and P-39 Airacobras were based at Fighter Two. The total number of serviceable fighters available for interception or escort duty averaged 100–120 on any given day by April 1943. (Matt Simek)

A flight of P-38s in very close formation, almost wingtip to wingtip. Had the Japanese timetable been pushed back just a few days, key members of the Yamamoto mission, including Lanphier and Barber, would have missed the opportunity to participate. The 70th Pursuit Squadron was scheduled to be rotated off Guadalcanal on April 17. After receiving the authorization from Halsey on April 16 to conduct the mission it was a personal call by Admiral Mitscher, on the recommendation of Colonel Pugh, that Lanphier and his flight, particularly, be held over in case they were needed. (NARA)

American fighters increasingly moved over to the offensive. On March 29, a mission comprising eight AAF P-38 Lightnings and eight Marine F-4U-1 Corsairs took off from Fighter Two to hit the Japanese floatplane base at the Shortland Islands. Flying in complete radio silence a few hundred feet above the water, this combined force did not take the direct route to its target but veered 50 miles west of New Georgia Island before heading north. By the time the flight reached the target area it had been whittled down by navigational and mechanical issues to just five P-38s and a single Corsair. Leading the force was newly promoted Captain Thomas G. Lanphier; his wingman was Lieutenant Rex T. Barber. Catching the Japanese aircraft on the water, the American pilots strafed them in turn, leaving seven of them burning at their moorings. As they turned for home, the US fighters encountered what they thought was a destroyer (but was later identified as a subchaser) and shot it up. Barber pressed home his attack run for a fraction of a second too long; as he pulled up, his P-38 got tangled with the ship's radio mast and he returned to Guadalcanal missing the last several feet of his left wingtip. Admiral Halsey subsequently cabled his congratulations, dubbing the mission "WORTH THE TRIP." For their roles, both Lanphier and Barber received the Oak Leaf Cluster to their previous awards of the Silver Star.

On April 17 the 18th Fighter Group, composed of the 6th and 19th Pursuit Squadrons, arrived at Guadalcanal via Fiji and Espíritu Santo to join the 347th as the second fighter group in the 13th Air Force. The fresh pilots were looking for action; they had no way of knowing they had arrived just in time to participate in an action of breathtaking scope and audacity.

THE PLAN

Yamamoto's fateful decision

The chain of events that culminated in the Yamamoto mission had been set in motion on December 7, 1941, at Pearl Harbor, but a decisive turning point was reached in the Japanese debacle at the battle of the Bismarck Sea, a running fight from March 3 to March 4, 1943, where American aircraft destroyed eight troop transports destined for New Guinea from Rabaul on New Britain Island, and sank four of eight accompanying destroyers.

The Allied victory again originated in intelligence. OP-20-G decrypts provided advance notice that the Japanese were setting up a schedule of convoys to the New Guinea ports of Lae, Madang, and Wewak in early March, specifying that the Lae convoy was delayed owing to the need to strengthen its escort of destroyers. CINCPAC was notified of which two Japanese Army divisions were earmarked for the operation (the 20th and 41st) and even had in hand an Eleventh Air Fleet message regarding air cover for the convoy which detailed the Lae convoy's size and timetable.

In addition, American tactics had evolved. As Army Air Force P-38s drove off the escorting Zeros, Boeing B-17s level-bombed from altitude while North American B-25s and Douglas A-20s used new low-level skip-bombing techniques to hammer the slow-moving ships below. The result was a complete, and, for the Allies, almost bloodless triumph.

With the tide of war clearly running against Japan, Yamamoto, headquartered at the great fleet base on Truk atoll in the Caroline Islands, resolved to take personal charge of the war effort in the Solomon Islands. Accompanied by his Chief of Staff, Matome Ugaki, and other key Combined Fleet administrative officers,

The business end of a P-38. The fighter's battery of four Browning M2 0.50in. machine guns and single Oldsmobile-manufactured Hispano M1 20mm cannon was concentrated in the nose to produce a tight circumference of fire not much larger than a basketball. Such clustering of all the armament in the nose was unusual in US aircraft, which typically used wing-mounted guns with trajectories set up to meet in a convergence zone. The rate of fire was approximately 650 rpm for the cannon and approximately 850 rpm for the machine guns. The combined rate of fire was over 4,000 rpm, with roughly every sixth projectile a 20mm shell. The duration of sustained firing for the 20mm cannon was approximately 14 seconds while the .50cal machine guns worked for 35 seconds if each magazine was fully loaded with 500 rounds. (NARA)

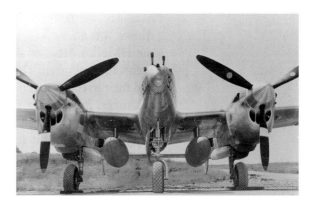

Yamamoto addresses his aircrews during Operation *I-Go*, Rabaul, 1943. This offensive was a desperate attempt to regain the initiative for Japan and restore credibility to a faltering grand strategic vision. As he had written to a correspondent congratulating him on his success at Pearl Harbor, "A military man can scarcely pride himself on having 'smitten a sleeping enemy'; it is more a matter of shame, simply, for the one smitten." He fully anticipated the United States, "angered and outraged," would lash back as soon as it was able. Accordingly, "my one desire is to carry through the first stage of operations before the enemy can recover, and, on the surface at least, achieve some basis for a protracted war." (Getty Images)

the Admiral and his entourage arrived at Rabaul via a pair of Emily flying boats on April 3. Never before had fleet headquarters been located ashore.

Wresting back the initiative would require a concentrated effort. The Japanese built up their airpower in the Solomons to an unprecedented three full JNAF flotillas, the Japanese adding *Kido Butai*'s air groups to the Rabaul base air force, though the flattops themselves remained at Truk.

On April 7, under the code name Operation *I-Go Sakusen*, Yamamoto unleashed his pilots on a series of massed raids against Guadalcanal and American bases in New Guinea. The stakes were high. Ugaki recorded in his diary the Combined Fleet had concluded that if the big offensive did not work, "[T]here will be no hope of future success in this area."

Two factors were working against Yamamoto. The first was the weather, which kept punctuating the rhythm of the offensive and deflating whatever momentum his pilots had achieved. The second was Allied intelligence, which kept his enemy always one step ahead of Japanese planning. As early as March 5 the CINCPAC fleet intelligence summary noted the movement from Japan to Rabaul of the 24th and 25th Air Flotillas. And the concentration of Japanese air power in the Solomons did not go unnoticed. Aerial reconnaissance and coastwatcher observation confirmed a massive expansion of the Japanese presence at Buin and Ballale.

On April 6, Ugaki, having received a report of an American cruiser-destroyer group headed for Munda or Kolombangara, described them in his diary as "good prey for our attack tomorrow." The following day, the Japanese sent 67 bombers escorted by 117 fighters winging toward Guadalcanal, but the Americans, forewarned, had already got the cruiser-destroyer group, which lay in Tulagi harbor, underway. COMAIRSOLS also ordered every available interceptor – 36 F4Fs, nine F4Us, 12 P-38s, 13 P-39s, and six P-40s – into the sky as an unprecedented warning, "Condition Very Red," went out for the first time in the Pacific War. By 1400hrs the Japanese were on radar. While the fighters mixed it up overhead, the Japanese bombers broke through to sink a destroyer, the USS *Aaron Ward*, a tanker, and, in an act of serendipitous revenge, a corvette, the HMNZS *Moa*, whose victory over the *I-1* had strongly affected the events that followed. This was meager compensation for the loss of aircraft and their irreplaceable pilots, however, as Japanese aircraft were shot down in droves. Rex Barber claimed two enemy fighters, while Tom Lanphier claimed three (which he accounted for in characteristically florid prose, describing how he put an "awesome burst of firepower" into one adversary "and blew him and his Zero into smithereens," while another "took the full power of my four machine guns in his belly and blew apart as he passed over my head").

The returns on raids of similar strength against Allied bases in New Guinea – Oro Bay on April 11, Port Moresby on April 12, and Milne Bay on April 14 – were similarly underwhelming, again at a severe cost in Japanese aircraft and crews. Yamamoto, who had stood beside the runway wearing his dress whites and waving his cap in farewell on every day of the offensive, called a halt on April 16. Declaring *I-Go* successfully concluded, he ordered the carrier planes back to Truk.

The next morning, Ugaki chaired a meeting at Rabaul to discuss the operation and its outcome. The mood was somber. Japanese freedom of action was now severely compromised by an ever-sharpening Allied edge in numbers, technology, and tactics. "The meeting concluded in a pessimistic air," Commander Okumiya of Carrier Division 2 recorded; "we could anticipate only expanding enemy air strength and an ever-increasing drain o[n] our own."

With logistics stretched to the limit, the tropical extremes were adding to the pressure on the Japanese. Ugaki was coming down with dengue fever; Southeast Area Fleet commander Kusaka Jinichi had dysentery; Yamamoto himself may have been suffering from beriberi, with swollen ankles and shaking hands, plus possible mental impairment. He was said to be changing his shoes four or five times a day and getting vitamin C shots from his doctor.

Nevertheless, Yamamoto was determined to fly to Ballale and Buin to congratulate his aviators personally. On Tuesday morning, April 13, Yamamoto decided to personally inspect frontline naval bases in the Shortland area, off the southern tip of Bougainville Island. His administrative officer, Commander Yasuji Watanabe, who had whiled away many evening hours at Rabaul playing shogi with Yamamoto, was tasked with working out the details of the itinerary.

Once drafted, the Admiral's itinerary was dispatched as a radio message from Southeast Area Fleet, Rabaul, that afternoon by Vice Admiral Tomoshiga Samejima, the commander of the Eighth Air Fleet. It read:

On 18 April Commander in Chief Combined Fleet will inspect Ballale, Shortland, and Buin as follows:
1. Depart Rabaul 0600 in medium attack plane escorted by six fighters, arrive Ballale 0800. Depart at once in subchaser to arrive Shortland 0840. Depart Shortland 0945 in subchaser to arrive Ballale 1030. Depart Ballale by plane to arrive Buin at 1110. Lunch at Buin. Depart Buin 1400 by plane to arrive Rabaul 1540.

The momentous message detailing Admiral Yamamoto's itinerary for his tour of the front line, as drafted by his administrative officer, Commander Yasuji Watanabe, paired with the partial decryption that sealed his fate. (Matt Simek)

Watanabe added such punctilious details as "Uniforms will be the uniform for the day except that the commanding officer of the various units will be in combat attire with decorations," and noting the entire excursion would be delayed 24 hours in the event of inclement weather. He had micromanaged the itinerary to the point of incorporating the extra time required on the return leg from Shortland via subchaser due to running against the tide. Almost the only detail he left out was to note the fleet staff's practice of putting the C-in-C and Chief of Staff in different aircraft so the top leadership would not all be wiped out in the event of a single plane crash.

Watanabe harbored doubts about the security of Army codes, so he ordered that the message be sent only in the Navy's D Code (JN-25). The dispatch went out late that afternoon. A subsequent inquiry revealed that – contrary to Watanabe's instructions – the message had gone out over both systems. Watanabe concluded the Army broadcast had been intercepted. In fact, while the message was written in a high-security cipher US codebreakers labeled JN25E14, this was valid only from January 3 through February 14 of that year. It's possible the old cipher was used for the April 13 communication because the newer version had not yet reached the Ballale base. Whatever the reason, the Allies now had an inside track on the dates, down to the minutes, of Yamamoto's future location. Unwittingly, Watanabe had just issued the Admiral's death warrant.

The decision to strike

It was confirmed Allied intelligence had opened a window into the heart of the enemy's command structure. But, now that US strategists knew they *could* target Yamamoto, the question emerged, *should* they do so? As Nimitz asked, "Do we try to get him?"

There were three considerations. First, would a mission specifically intended to result in the death of an individual, Admiral Yamamoto, be considered legitimate under the rules of war, or would it constitute a form of political assassination? Second, was there a risk the death of Yamamoto might backfire by elevating a more dangerous adversary as enemy C-in-C? And third, if US fighters showed up out of the blue at exactly the right place and time to take down their highest-ranking officer, the Japanese might finally realize their codes were compromised and take action that could black out the access Allied intelligence had been enjoying for over a year. Was eliminating Yamamoto worth the risk of exposing this trump card?

Nimitz was apparently disinterested in the first question, and sanguine about the third. He and Layton, who knew Yamamoto personally and professionally, discussed the implications for the IJN of losing him. So far as Layton saw it, there was no substitute. "He's unique among their people … Aside from the Emperor, probably no man in Japan is so important to civilian morale." His absence "would demoralize the fighting navy. You know Japanese psychology; it would stun the nation." He then resorted to blatant sycophancy in order to sell his point. "You know, Admiral Nimitz, it would be just as if they shot you down. There isn't anybody to replace you." Nimitz smiled, probably amused despite himself. "It's down in Halsey's

The decryption (overleaf)

FRUPAC and Negat had picked up Watanabe's message almost as soon as its intended recipient, and FRUMEL obtained a later retransmission as well as the text recirculated by US intelligence on the Copek circuit. Cryptanalysts at Pearl Harbor and in Washington immediately appreciated they had intercepted a communication of critical significance. Though the Imperial Navy had changed its additive table on April 1, complicating work with JN-25, many values had already been recovered, especially oft-repeated terms like names of commands and places. Lieutenant Roger Pineau at FRUPAC later recorded that the large number of addressees for Watanabe's dispatch had instantly drawn attention; "We've hit the jackpot!" Marine Major Alva B. "Red" Lasswell exclaimed.

At FRUPAC, cryptanalysts Tommy Dyer and "Ham" Wright worked to recover new additives and code groups, traffic analysts like Tom Huckins and Jack Williams reworked the addressee information, and "Jasper" Holmes' estimates section searched for area designators. Through their efforts the code groups of the underlying message were revealed. By this stage of the war the codebreakers were using new technology, IBM mechanical card-sorting machines, to help break messages. Each code group in a message would be punched onto a card, and the sorter would run the cards against another set containing known JN-25 meanings. RR was Rabaul; RXZ was Ballale, an island off the southern tip of Bougainville; RXP was Buin, a nearby base on Bougainville Island. Experts filled in the remaining gaps by evaluating their context relative to sentences in other messages. Once a basic version of the original (the "plaintext") had been recovered, it was ready for the language experts, in this case Lasswell and Lieutenant Commander John G. Roenigk.

The same process played out in Washington. At Negat, Lieutenant Commander Prescott Currier had the predawn watch when the intercept arrived. He took it to the "Blitz Additive Room." In the morning, Commander Redfield "Rosie" Mason assigned linguists Phillip Cate, Dorothy Edgars, and Fred Woodrough to make the translation, insisting, "I want every damned date, time, and place checked and double-checked."

FRUPAC won this race, sending out a dispatch to COMINCH, CINCPAC, COMSOPAC, and the commander of the 7th Fleet at 1008hrs on Wednesday, April 14, reporting its preliminary findings in decoding the Japanese message intercepted the previous day. The decryption was truncated and fragmentary, but it had cracked three key elements – a date, a location, and, most significantly, an individual, none less than the Commander-in-Chief of the Imperial Combined Fleet, Admiral Yamamoto himself:

> On 18 April CINC COMBINED FLEET will … as follows: Ballale Island …

"This is probably a schedule of inspection by CINC COMBINED FLEET," FRUPAC commented. "The message lacks additives, but work will be continued on it."

Later that same day, FRUPAC was able to send out a more complete translation of the same message:

> In accordance with the following schedule CINC COMBINED FLEET will be at Ballale and Buin on 18 April:
>
> 1. In a medium attack plane escorted by six fighters depart Rabaul at 0600. At 0800 (1000 'L' time) arrive Ballale. Proceed by minesweeper to … arriving at 0840. At # Base have minesweeper ready to proceed to … arriving at 0840. At 0945 depart … in minesweeper and arrive at 1030 at Ballale. In a medium attack plane depart Buin at 1400 and arrive at 1540 at Rabaul.

Lieutenant Donald M. Showers plotted the itinerary and measured times and distances on maps to verify plausibility. Everything checked out.

Lasswell first shared this decrypt by secure scrambler telephone with Jasper Holmes. In this plate, Lasswell and Holmes meet in the "Dungeon" of Station Hypo to confirm one last time the accuracy of the decryption. Satisfied, they delivered the translation by hand to Commander Edwin T. Layton, Admiral Chester W. Nimitz's intelligence officer, who then took it directly to his superior. Meeting with Nimitz shortly after 0800hrs, Layton simply handed him the dispatch and said, "Our old friend Yamamoto."

"I am looking forward to dictating peace to the United States in the White House at Washington"
— ADMIRAL YAMAMOTO

What do YOU say, AMERICA?

This poster, intended to mobilize American opinion against Yamamoto in the wake of Pearl Harbor, is based on a willfully deceptive translation of his actual statement. The Admiral had in fact issued a challenge to his superiors that if they were to choose war with the United States, "then our aim, of course, ought not to be Guam or the Philippines, nor Hawaii or Hong Kong, but a capitulation at the White House, in Washington itself. I wonder whether the politicians of the day really have the willingness to make sacrifices, and the confidence, that this would entail." The American public was not privy to such nuance, however; Tom Lanphier could speak for main street when he described Yamamoto as "a conceited and arrogant man, with a face like a frog, an easy man to hate. For in his malevolent person he contained such power for evil." (NARA)

bailiwick," he replied. "If there's a way, he'll find it. All right, we'll try it."

On April 15, CINCPAC issued a daily Ultra Bulletin to all Task Force Commanders in the Pacific, notifying them:

At 1000 on 18 April YAMAMOTO himself, via bomber escorted by six fighters, will arrive from Rabaul in the Ballale-Shortland area.
He will leave Kahili at 1600 the same day and return to Rabaul.

Independent confirmation was achieved later that day when FRUMEL disseminated to COMINCH, CINCPAC, COMSOPAC and the commander of the 7th Fleet the decryption of another Japanese message from Rabaul, dated April 14, possibly one of the dispatches that had concerned Admiral Joshima, making reference to "the special visit of Yamamoto," which, "in view of the situation regarding air attacks on the post," necessitated precautionary measures, including relocation of the post to a more secure location. The message contained the suggestions, "Give consideration to construction of slit trenches and other defense devices" and "Cause the 13 millimeter machine guns to be brought up." Attached to the decryption was a comment by the unknown cryptographer who forwarded the message: CATCH HIM IN THE AIR.

The CINCPAC war diary for April 16 records that "an attempt will be made to intercept an enemy high commander when he makes a projected visit to the Buin area the 18th." Layton subsequently prepared a top-secret message to Halsey for Nimitz's approval that emphasized the need for operational secrecy in order to protect, as far as possible, the cryptanalysis breakthrough that had set the process in motion:

BELIEVE SPECIFIC EFFORT WORTHWHILE.
IN ORDER PROTECT R.I. [Radio Intelligence] SUGGEST PILOTS BE TOLD COASTWATCHER RABAUL AREA SIGNALLED OUR SUB TO EFFECT UNKNOWN HIGH RANKING OFFICER MAKING TRIP TO BALLALE OR SOME SUCH SOURCE
SUGGEST EVERY EFFORT BE MADE TO MAKE OPERATION APPEAR FORTUITOUS
IF FORCES YOUR COMMAND HAVE CAPABILITY SHOOT DOWN YAMAMOTO AND STAFF, YOU ARE HEREBY AUTHORIZED INITIATE PRELIMINARY PLANNING
OUR BEST WISHES AND HIGH HOPES GO WITH THOSE INTERCEPTING HUNTERS

Nimitz approved the message but added a personal note for Halsey:

BEST OF LUCK AND GOOD HUNTING

Admiral William F. Halsey, Commander, South Pacific, who had stated on numerous occasions that Yamamoto was "No. 3 on my private list of public enemies, closely trailing Hirohito and Tojo," seized on this breakthrough with relish. He informed his subordinate task force commanders, Admiral Aubrey Fitch, Commander, Air, South Pacific (COMAIRSOPAC), and Admiral Marc A. "Pete" Mitscher, Commander, Air, Solomons (COMAIRSOLS), located on Guadalcanal:

INDICATOR JAPS TO HOLD CONFERENCE SOON CONCERNING OPERATIONS AND DEFENSE MEASURES FOR NEW GUINEA SOLOMONS BISMARK AREA ...
YAMAMOTO HIMSELF ARRIVING BALLALE SHORTLAND AREA AT 10 HOURS ON 18TH VIA BOMBER FROM RABAUL
ESCORTED BY 6 FIGHTERS
TO RETURN RABAUL (WE HOPE NOT) DEPARTING KAHILI 16 HOURS SAME DAY

If the three bracketed words didn't make Halsey's intentions clear enough, he appended the comment:

TALLEYHO [sic]
LET'S GET THE BASTARD

Yamamoto's field command on Rabaul was headquartered in this bunker. While tropical diseases made the island problematic for Japanese personnel stationed there, the volcanic ash on Rabaul made it a less than optimal operational environment for the aircraft they were flying. During August 1942 the JNAF would lose 214 planes in combat and 138 more in accidents. The figures for September were 113 combat against 123 operational losses, commencing a trend that would only worsen as the war continued and more and more undertrained and inexperienced Japanese aircrews were rushed into the front lines. (Getty Images)

One enduring question about the Yamamoto mission is how far up the chain of command authorization extended. Nimitz presumably shared the details of the plan as it unfolded with his superior in Washington, Admiral Ernest J. King, Commander-in-Chief, US Fleet, but there is no indication that King ever approved, let alone was involved in directing, the mission. The same can be said for Secretary of the Navy Frank Knox. Several individuals involved with operational planning at the April 17 meeting on Guadalcanal swore they saw Knox's signature on the authorization to proceed with the mission. Lanphier, in particular, recalled the message, titled TOP SECRET, was typed out on blue-colored tissue paper that appeared to be an original printout directly from a teletype machine. According to Lanphier, it read:

SQUADRON 339 P-38 MUST AT ALL COST REACH AND DESTROY
PRESIDENT ATTACHES EXTREME IMPORTANCE TO THIS OPERATION

The message was signed, "KNOX."

However, Lanphier, as will be discussed, was an unreliable witness. Furthermore, Knox had no authority over Army air units, and US security

Marc "Pete" Mitscher (left) began the war as captain of USS *Hornet*; it was from the decks of this carrier that Jimmy Doolittle's 16 B-25 bombers set off for their raid on Tokyo, April 18, 1942. The *Hornet* was one of three US carriers in action at Midway less than two months later. Having been promoted to Admiral, Mitscher took over as Commander Air, Solomon Islands (COMAIRSOLS) on Guadalcanal at the beginning of April, 1943. Chester Nimitz was selected by President Franklin D. Roosevelt to be Commander-in-Chief, United States Pacific Fleet (CINCPACFLT) and promoted to Admiral after the Japanese attack on Pearl Harbor. Drawing on the information made available by his intelligence assets, he coolly deployed the limited resources available to him throughout 1942 to blunt the Japanese impetus at the Coral Sea, Midway, and the Solomon Islands, before rolling the enemy back all the way to Tokyo Bay over the next three years. (NARA)

practice strictly prohibited incorporating codebreaking information in an operational message.

Did authorization originate from the Commander-in-Chief himself? President Franklin D. Roosevelt had left the White House via train on the afternoon of April 13 for an inspection tour of military installations and defense plants in the southwest, en route to an address in Monterrey, Mexico, to boost hemispheric solidarity. The last official record of consultation between him and Knox was on April 9, five days prior to the intelligence breakthrough. In fact, there are no official records of direct contact between Knox and Roosevelt from April 13 until April 18, when a dispatch from the White House Map Room reported P-38s had shot down three bombers the previous day (Guadalcanal time). A second dispatch received April 19 suggested "the possibility that Admiral Yamamoto may have been in one of the bombers shot down."

Researchers have combed the Naval Archives, the National Archives, and the FDR Library at Hyde Park but found no "smoking gun" document proving Roosevelt's approval for the mission was requested, or, in fact, that any communication on this subject ever took place between Nimitz and any of his superiors in Washington. On balance, "There seems little reason to doubt that Nimitz, at his own level, made the decision to get Yamamoto, and higher authority did not impede him," John Prados concludes. That is a significant departure from contemporary practice, where interdictions of high-profile individuals are micromanaged directly from the White House. But, "The world was simpler then."

American planning

On April 16, Rear Admiral Marc A. Mitscher, who had just taken command of air operations in the Solomons (COMAIRSOLS) on April 1, received authorization from Halsey to begin planning for the Yamamoto mission: "The peacock will be on time. Fan his tail." He requested his Chief of Staff, General Field Harris (USMC), and Assistant Chief of Staff for Operations, Commander Stanley C. Ring (USN), to meet him in his cabin, where the two officers were informed about the contents of the dispatch. All present agreed that a conference should be held immediately with additional ranking Navy and Marine officers to discuss possible means of interception.

At this second, expanded conference, Mitscher, Harris, and Ring were joined by Assistant Chief of Staff for Administration Commander William A. Read (USNR); Fighter Command OIC Lieutenant Colonel Edwin L. Pugh (USMC); Pugh's assistant, Lieutenant Colonel L. Samuel Moore (USMC); and Fighter Command Operations Officer Major John P. Condon (USMC). Significantly, the only representative of the Army Air Force present was Lieutenant Colonel Aaron W. Tyer, base commander on

Fighter Two. The first instinct of the Navy was to keep the opportunity of eliminating Yamamoto as in-house as possible.

The conclave deliberated over the timeframe and geographic parameters of Yamamoto's itinerary to the last detail. Ultimately, all concerned were confronted by the inescapable fact that the Navy's F4F and F4U fighters did not possess the range necessary to carry out a successful interception. Accepting that only the Army's P-38s had this capability, Mitscher set aside any inter-service rivalry and called for 13th Fighter Command Assistant OIC and 347th Group Commander Lieutenant Colonel Henry Viccellio (AAF) to join the discussion. Once informed of the mission parameters, Viccellio had no hesitation in settling on his strike group commander.

Major John W. Mitchell, the newly appointed commander of the 339th Fighter Squadron, was lying on a cot in his headquarters tent on Guadalcanal's Fighter Two airstrip trying to snatch some sleep between missions, when Viccellio poked his head under the tent flap: "Mitch, they want you over at the Opium Den at Henderson. They've got something for you."

Mitchell and Viccellio drove to the pilots' bivouac area to pick up Major Louis Kittel, the newly arrived commander of the 12th Fighter Squadron. Viccellio and Mitchell told the group of pilots lounging around to lay off the drinking that night because they had a big mission coming up the next day. Just as they started to pull away, Viccellio called out to Captain Thomas G. Lanphier, of the 70th Fighter Squadron, "Why don't you go with us over to Henderson because you'll probably be on it." Lanphier nodded and got aboard.

Debate in the dugout (overleaf)

When they arrived, the small, stuffy dugout was crowded with Navy, Marine, and Army officers clustered around the large planning table in the center of the room. In Lanphier's account, every "brass hat" on the island was there and they had to elbow their way in.

Over the course of the ensuing discussion, "a lot of people who weren't going on the mission had a lot to say, but as usual in a crowd like this there's always a bunch of big mouths, and so quite a hassle developed," Mitchell recalled. There was "much discussion … a lot of arguments." Navy personnel, noting that Yamamoto was scheduled to arrive in Bougainville via submarine tender after landing at Ballale, proposed ambushing him in transit. Their key point was that the time it would take for Yamamoto to arrive at the seaplane base on Shortland would allow for greater flexibility in the mission, as the pilots would have a much better chance of locating and hitting a slow-moving target on the water than a fast-moving target in the air.

When one of the conferees began mapping out the mission in nautical terms, Mitchell finally interrupted: "'Port quarter,' what the hell does that mean! Listen, I honestly can't tell you the difference between a subchaser and a sub. What if there are several boats? What if the guy can swim? No, this doesn't make sense." Additionally, there was the question of the Japanese fighters based at Kahili. "We would have to be over the target too long trying to get in trail to strafe a boat in the water. If they sent up fighters to escort the Admiral, we'd be in a poor position to defend ourselves at such a low altitude and still get any hits on the target, assuming we could identify it in the first place." In Mitchell's account, he finally paused and stared directly at Mitscher. "We're fighter pilots. We should take him in the air!" The room fell silent. Mitscher then settled the issue by coming down firmly on the side of his strike group commander. "Mitchell's got to do the job, let's do it his way."

According to Condon, Mitscher ended the debate by remarking "we have discussed all these alternatives long enough," and left the final call to Mitchell: "He's going to make the flight. He should make the choice." Mitchell now had the authority to impose his preferred option, making the interception in the air, because "if it's made, it's a sure thing. I mean, if we shoot that plane down, nobody is going to survive."

When Mitchell and his fellow pilots turned for the door, heading back to the Opium Den, Mitscher stopped them and asked, "Is there anything else you need from us?" Mitchell had one request: "A compass, one of those big Navy jobs installed on the ships." From personal experience, he was only too aware the compasses in the P-38 weren't reliable and couldn't be trusted because they couldn't be swung properly. Pilots had learned the only time their equipment was anywhere near accurate was when they lined up for takeoff because then they knew the runway heading. Mitscher nodded, "You got it." As Mitchell later put it, "thank God that we had an admiral that could see my point of view, because I'm sure the mission wouldn't have been a success if we had done it any other way."

From Castelton, North Dakota, Major Louis Kittel, commander of the 12th FS, is depicted in this formal portrait not sporting the thick beard that would be his trademark while serving in the distinctly less formal environs of Guadalcanal. Innovative and something of a nonconformist, Kittel would prove himself a specialist in night fighting, winning the DFC in recognition of this proficiency. "Major Kittel got into the searchlights at night one time and you could hear a roar all over the island when he flamed a couple of Bettys up there," one contemporary recalled "Two in one night. God, it was just like a standing ovation on that island, no less!" (Matt Simek)

Once the decision for an airborne interception had been made (see plate commentary), the AAF representatives adjourned to the Fighter Command dugout, where the mechanics of the strike were discussed around the map table. Mitchell, Lanphier, Pugh, Viccellio, and Condon were joined by Fighter Command Assistant OIC Lieutenant Colonel L. Samuel Moore (USMC) and Fighter Command Intelligence Officer Lieutenant P. Lewis (USNR). Estimates were laid out concerning course, speed, and altitude to the Kahili area, point of anticipated interception, the weather forecast (clear, with haze limiting visibility to a few miles over the water), Japanese AA and fighter defenses on Bougainville, and the return flight to Guadalcanal. After studying a map, Mitchell concluded, "we ought to back everything up so that the intercept, if it happens, will take place about right here," indicating just south of Empress Augusta Bay. The pilots then went back to Fighter Two to get flight preparations in motion.

Viccellio ordered the maintenance crews to get the 18 available P-38s ready for launch in the morning. These were fitted for two external fuel tanks, but with a maximum capacity of 165 gallons each – not enough fuel to reach Bougainville, accomplish the mission, and return to base. The fighters were compatible with 310-gallon fuel tanks, but only General Kenney's 5th Air Force, affiliated with MacArthur's SOWESPAC in New Guinea, had any of these available. Guadalcanal had been waiting for delivery of these tanks for weeks; Viccellio now sent out an urgent request for their arrival to be expedited for that evening.

Condon, meanwhile, sat down at the table to plot the courses and air speeds that had to be maintained to work the intercept selected, based on Yamamoto's schedule. After cross-checking his figures with Pugh at Fighter

The P-38 was a versatile weapon that offered a platform suitable for interception, dive-bombing, level bombing, ground attack, night fighting, photo reconnaissance, radar and visual pathfinding for bombers, and evacuation missions. Its forte was as a long-range escort fighter when equipped with drop tanks under its wings. (NARA)

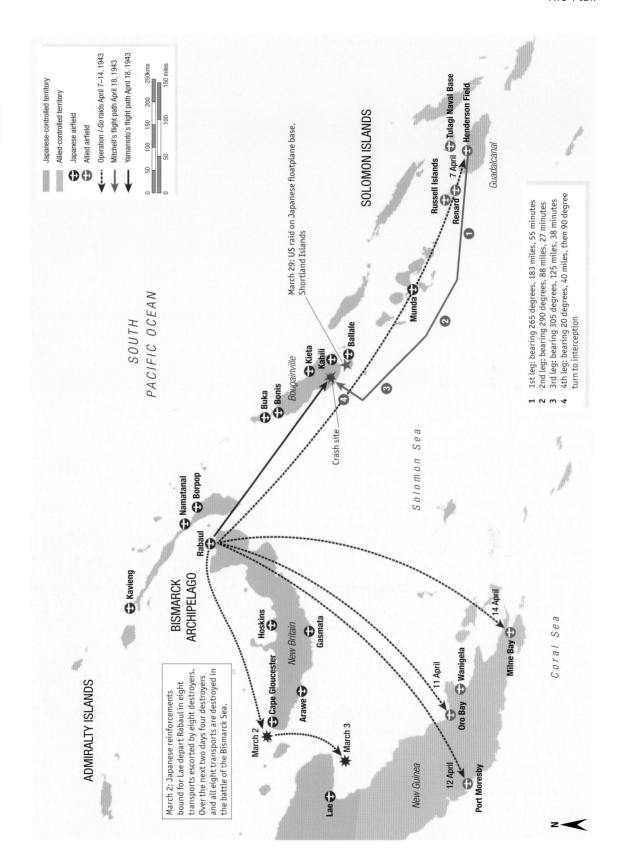

ADMIRALTY ISLANDS

SOUTH
PACIFIC OCEAN

BISMARCK
ARCHIPELAGO

SOLOMON ISLANDS

Solomon Sea

Coral Sea

New Guinea

Kavieng

Namatanal
Borpop
Rabaul

Buka
Bonis
Bougainville
Kieta
Kahili
Ballale

Crash site

March 29: US raid on Japanese floatplane base,
Shortland Islands

Munda

Russell Islands
Renard
Tulagi Naval Base
Henderson Field
Guadalcanal
7 April

Hoskins
Cape Gloucester
Arawe
Gasmata
New Britain

March 2
March 3

Lae
Port Moresby
12 April
Wanigela
Oro Bay
11 April
14 April
Milne Bay

Legend:
- Japanese-controlled territory
- Allied-controlled territory
- Japanese airfield
- Allied airfield
- Operation *I-Go* raids April 7–14, 1943
- Mitchell's flight path April 18, 1943
- Yamamoto's flight path April 18, 1943

0   50   100   150   200   250kms
0   50   100   150   miles

March 2: Japanese reinforcements
bound for Lae depart Rabaul in eight
transports escorted by eight destroyers.
Over the next two days four destroyers
and all eight transports are destroyed in
the battle of the Bismarck Sea.

1 1st leg: bearing 265 degrees, 183 miles, 55 minutes
2 2nd leg: bearing 290 degrees, 88 miles, 27 minutes
3 3rd leg: bearing 305 degrees, 125 miles, 38 minutes
4 4th leg: bearing 20 degrees, 40 miles, then 90 degree
   turn to interception

N

The unique twin-boom construction of the P-38 is shown to advantage in this photo, clearly illustrating the rationale behind the nickname given to the Lightning by its Japanese adversaries: Two Fighters, One Pilot. Lockheed designed the P-38 in response to a February 1937 specification from the United States Army Air Corps calling for a maximum airspeed of at least 360mph at altitude and a climb to 20,000ft within six minutes. The twin-engine, twin-boom design was the novel solution to these stringent requirements arrived at by the design team at Lockheed under Clarence 'Kelly' Johnson and Hall Hibbard. (NARA)

Command headquarters, the data was presented on a strip map with the mission's course and the airspeed, distance, and time computed to Mitchell at Fighter Two by Lieutenant Joseph E. McGuigan, a navy intelligence officer, and Captain William Morrison, his army counterpart. Mitchell laid out a map of the Solomon Islands on a table in the mess tent and studied it by lamplight.

Mitchell didn't trust the airspeed, distance, and time figures in Condon's proposed mission parameters. Condon didn't fly the Air Force P-38s; he didn't know the indicated airspeed Mitchell would set his throttles for long-range cruise, or what altitude Mitchell planned to fly. "If I had followed Condon's route, we would have been 40 to 50 miles offshore from where I wanted to be," Mitchell later recalled.

Starting from scratch, Mitchell labored over the map while McGuigan and Morrison carefully drew lines and double-checked his figures. First, he estimated Yamamoto's bomber's speed to be 180mph, or three miles a minute, presuming the bomber was to be a Navy G4M Betty rather than the older Army K-21 Sally. This assumption made sense, given Yamamoto was an Admiral, but was no more than "Strictly a guess," Mitchell later commented, "because no one seemed to know for sure."

He computed the P-38's zero wind ground speed under long-range cruise control settings to be 200mph. He then recalculated the average speed to target as 197mph, having been informed the flight would have a quartering wind at between five to ten knots off its port bow on the first leg. As he put it, "this is navy language, but anyhow I had a pretty good idea of what they were talking about so I cranked it into my schedule."

Since a direct flight to Bougainville meant crossing or flying close to Japanese-held islands and enemy observers on islands along the way up the Slot from Fighter Two, the flight would have to veer far out to sea to avoid visual contact by Japanese coastwatchers, and skim the ocean at wave-top height to avoid detection by Japanese radar. Mitchell plotted the mission's course to remain at least 50 miles offshore. On the outbound route there would be no landmarks to use as checkpoints; it would have to be dead reckoning all the way, flying only by airspeed, clock, and compass in complete radio silence for two hours over 400 miles of water at 50 feet or less until landfall off the Bougainville coast.

Mitchell knew Yamamoto's arrival time at Ballale, but did not know over which side of Bougainville Yamamoto's bomber would fly. He predicted Yamamoto would fly the direct route from Rabaul down the western coast, and calculated the best intercept point to be about 30 miles, or approximately ten minutes' flying time for the bomber, which would be in its approach to the airfield, descending from about 5,000ft at that point. Since the Admiral was due at Ballale at 0945hrs, the interception should take place at 0935hrs Guadalcanal time, 0735hrs Japanese time.

Mitchell divided his flight plan into five legs. Working backward from 0935 Guadalcanal time, he calculated that takeoff from Guadalcanal would have to be at 0720. Allowing 15 minutes for join-up in formation, the flight should depart the island area at 0735 Guadalcanal time.

Even with the external fuel tanks, the P-38s would still be at the extreme limit of their range. Mitchell estimated once they arrived over Buin his fighters would have no more than 15 minutes in which to target Yamamoto's plane and complete the mission. At the time, "I figured the odds at about a thousand to one that we could make a successful intercept at that distance," Mitchell later confessed; "Today, after years of thinking about it, I'd make that a million to one."

The one thing Mitchell couldn't factor into his planning was the human element. There were no guarantees Yamamoto wouldn't change his mind at the last minute to delay his departure, change the itinerary, or cancel the trip altogether.

> The only assurance we had was from Captain Morrison, the army intelligence officer who had lived in Japan for a number of years. He reiterated a number of times that the Japanese were noted for their punctuality and that Yamamoto was well known publicly for keeping precise schedules, that it was an obsession with him. He said the one thing we could count on was that Yamamoto would be on time.

Selecting the pilots for the mission became problematic, "for soon the word got out about what we were going to do. A fistfight almost broke out on a couple of occasions" among pilots arguing their respective merits for inclusion. "Everybody wanted to go," Mitchell said. "If there was going to be a big show, they all wanted in on it – typical fighter pilots." Word of the mission, and the name of its intended target, was spreading like wildfire across Guadalcanal; according to Condon, "the whole bloody island eventually knew who it was sooner or later."

Mitchell went down the list of about 40 pilots available and chose the final 18. They were men he had flown with from Fiji and New Caledonia with the 12th and 70th Fighter Squadrons and who were now assigned to the newly

A6M Model 22 (Zero) fighters from the IJN aircraft carrier *Zuikaku*'s air group stationed at Buin, Bougainville in early 1943. The Zero had ruled the skies over the western Pacific in the six months after Pearl Harbor, but during the protracted attritional struggle for the Solomon Islands it was eclipsed by next-generation American rivals. "The Japanese airplanes just blow up if you get a good burst into them with the P-38's four guns in the nose," one American report concluded; "they will burn with one burst if you hit them correctly around the wing root or the cockpit. It will either explode or get the pilot. They are just like tissue paper." (Imperial Japanese Navy/Public domain)

activated 339th under his command. All three squadrons were assigned to the 347th Fighter Group headed by Viccellio.

Mitchell assigned four aircraft to the "killer flight" that would be tasked with intercepting and eliminating Yamamoto's aircraft. This was to avoid congestion and confusion in the target area. As Mitchell explained, there was "no way that I wanted 18 airplanes up there milling around trying to shoot down one bomber." The other 14 P-38s would fly Combat Air Patrol (CAP) above the killer flight to hold off any fighters the Japanese were able to scramble while the interception was in progress. In making this tactical disposition, Mitchell was displaying implicit faith in the combat prowess of the men selected for his killer flight, who he assumed would be able to focus on and destroy Yamamoto's aircraft despite being outnumbered by the Japanese escort fighters; "we knew they had six Zeros up, but that didn't really concern us that much either."

According to Mitchell, "Lou Kittel was on my back all the time trying to get a bunch of his men in there, for he was in another squadron with experienced P-38 pilots. He had some good crews and so we couldn't afford to leave them out, so he selected some of his people and I selected the others." Ultimately, Mitchell let Kittel select seven other men besides himself to fly in the cover flight. Mitchell's selection criteria were simple; "after you have flown with those people for a number of missions, you get to know them, and you know who you can depend on."

Mitchell continued working by lantern and flashlight until he was sure his calculations were correct. When he finished, he spread the word that he wanted all 339th pilots to be awakened at 0500hrs, get breakfast, and report to the operations tent at 0600 for a briefing.

That evening, the long-range drop tanks arrived at Henderson aboard B-24 heavy bombers from the 90th Bomb Group at Port Moresby, New Guinea, and were trucked to Fighter Two. While Mitchell slept, ground crews worked frantically throughout the night, sheltering from torrential rainfall under tarpaulins in the revetments. In the event, there were just enough to go around for one to be fitted to each P-38, so the pilots would have to take off balancing one 165-gallon tank and one 310-gallon tank. As they were fueled, the fighters were also being armed; the 20mm cannon were loaded with HE incendiary shells, and the four .50cal machine guns were loaded with a mixture of tracer, API, and ball ammunition.

The weather was fine when Mitchell arose at 0430, ate a light breakfast, and rechecked his flight plan. When the pilots assembled, he told them the essentials of the task the squadron had been assigned, confirmed who the target was, and reminded them the mission was highly classified. "I told them it was to be an all-volunteer mission and, as I expected, everyone kept asking if they could go," Mitchell said. He listed the names of the pilots he had selected on a blackboard and informed them the flight would be cruising for two hours at about 200mph indicated airspeed. They were "to fly off of my lead, stay awake, and not to fixate on the water, which is easy to do on a long mission so close to the waves."

Ray Hine graduated with a degree in civil engineering from Purdue University, but his real love was 19th-century Gothic literature, judging by his call sign – Heathcliff, the brooding antihero of Emily Brontë's *Wuthering Heights*. Having signed up as an air cadet while still a student, he was awarded his wings five days after Pearl Harbor. Hine had served for several months at Guadalcanal when he took off as wingman to Besby Holmes on April 18, 1943, but all his previous combat experience was in the P-40 Warhawk. That day was his first mission in a P-38 – and his last. (Matt Simek)

US PERSONNEL

347th Fighter Group

First Flight (High Cover)

Maj. John Mitchell, 339FS CO,
Mission Leader
1st Lt. Julius Jacobson,
339FS, Wingman
1st Lt. Douglas Canning, 339FS,
Element Leader
1st Lt. Delton Goerke,
339FS, Wingman

Spare Element

1st Lt. Besby Holmes, 339FS,
Element Leader
1st Lt. Raymond Hine,
339FS, Wingman

Second Flight (Attack)

Capt. Thomas Lanphier, Jr., 70th
Fighter Squadron, Section Leader
1st Lt. Rex Barber, 339FS, Wingman

1st Lt. Joseph Moore, 70FS,
Element Leader
1st Lt. James McLanahan,
339FS, Wingman

18th Fighter Group

First Flight (High Cover)

Maj. Louis Kittel, 12FS, Acting CO,
Section Leader
2nd Lt. Gordon Whittaker,
12FS, Wingman
1st Lt. Roger Ames, 12FS,
Element Leader
1st Lt. Lawrence Graebner,
12FS, Wingman

Second Flight (High Cover)

1st Lt. Everett Anglin, 12FS,
Section Leader
1st Lt. William Smith, 12FS, Wingman
1st Lt. Eldon Stratton, 12FS,
Element Leader
1st Lt. Albert Long, 12FS, Wingman

Mitchell notified them he would use the usual signals of kicking his rudders to fishtail his plane when he wanted the formation to spread out, and wagging his wings when he wanted them to close up. He would use hand signals otherwise. "I won't surprise you with any sharp turns," he promised.

After making landfall at Bougainville they would jettison their drop tanks, at which point the killer section of four aircraft would seek out the bomber and the six fighters while the others would climb rapidly to provide cover and also be ready to intercept any of the 75 to 100 Zeros based at Kahili that got airborne. This was a preoccupation for Mitchell, who "anticipated a real turkey shoot" over Bougainville.

> I really expected them to send up at least 50 of those fighters … Guess I was being greedy but I felt sure they would greet their top boss with a big show of an escort force and we'd be able to pounce on them from altitude. I thought we were going to be in for a hell of a good fight and I didn't want to miss it.

In addition, he didn't want 18 P-38s contesting against only six escorting Zeros and a lone bomber. "That way, there would be too many trying to get the bomber and we would be getting in each other's way."

The interior of a P-38 cockpit, featuring the instrument panel. In another distinct feature, the aircraft was controlled by a yoke as opposed to the stick prevalent in most US fighters. The P-38 was overshadowed by the P-47 Thunderbolt and P-51 Mustang in the European theater, but found its niche in the wide open expanse of the Pacific, especially after it was upgraded in June 1942 from the P-38F to the P-38G, the newer variant boasting a pair of the more powerful 1,400hp (1,000 kW) Allison engines. Pilots flying the Lightning destroyed more Japanese planes in the war than those flying any other American aircraft. (NARA)

Mitchell selected Tom Lanphier to head the killer section of four aircraft. The other three were Rex Barber, Jim McLanahan, and Joe Moore. Besby Holmes and Ray Hine were designated spares and were to fill into any position in the formation for a pilot who had trouble and had to turn back. "If anyone had to abort, I told them to move up in their respective formations by hand signals only. No one was to touch that mike button from the time we took off until we engaged the enemy planes."

Finally, Mitchell emphasized to his pilots they were to make directly for Guadalcanal when the mission was completed; "We were not going to shoot up the fighter strip at Kahili or attack any other targets on the ground or water," because they wouldn't have the fuel to linger over the target area. The mission objective was simple: "we were to get that bomber no matter what. That was it."

The briefing concluded on that note. The pilots were all given small strip maps and copies of Mitchell's flight plan with the headings and times for each leg listed. Mitchell urged each pilot to check the drop tank installations on their fighters during their preflight walk-arounds and switch to them soon after takeoff to be sure they would feed. "There were a few questions but these boys were all well-trained and experienced," Mitchell related. "I had the utmost confidence in all of them. If anybody could do the job, I knew they could."

As the pilots dispersed to their fighters, Mitchell strode briskly down the line of P-38s, exchanging a few words with the mechanics and other personnel in the revetments along the flight line. After confirming with his own crew chief all systems were go, Mitchell climbed up on the wing of his Lightning, buckled his parachute leg straps, and eased into the cockpit. He checked the installation of the large navy compass and started the twin Allison engines. Acting on his engine start, the other 17 pilots cranked up and followed him out to the run-up position. After checking both engines carefully, Mitchell lined up on the runway. He paused to check the compass to see if it read the same as the runway heading. "It was right on the money," he noted. "So I knew it was going to be all right – certainly an improvement over my regular compass. It made me feel better about flying the courses out." If the wind stayed light as predicted, he was confident about his chances of getting to Bougainville sight unseen and on time. All that remained was for Admiral Yamamoto to do his part. So, at 0710hrs, April 18, the longest aerial interception mission of World War II commenced.

THE MISSION

Mitchell, in P-38 No. 110, held the brakes as he revved both engines up to full rpms; he released the brakes, checked the compass alignment with the runway heading once more, and was quickly airborne, initiating a slow left climbing turn to 2,000ft. He was followed by Lieutenant Julius Jacobson, his wingman, in No. 144, then Lieutenants Doug Canning, Delton Goerke, Besby Holmes (in No. 100), and Ray Hine (in No. 102). Next in line was the four-plane "killer" flight. Captain Tom Lanphier was in No. 122 ("Phoebe," the nickname for his fiancée and future wife, Phyllis). He was followed by Lieutenants Rex Barber in No. 147 ("Miss Virginia"), James D. McLanahan, and Joseph F. Moore. Lou Kittel was flying No. 125 ("Daisy 2"); Barber had damaged the port wing of this aircraft during his attack on a Japanese subchaser on March 29th, but it had been repaired in time for the mission with a wing cannibalized from No. 138 ("Old Ironsides").

One constant in warfare is contingency. Even the most meticulously planned special operations can be aborted (Desert One, 1980) or nearly founder (*Neptune's Spear*, 2011) because of mechanical failures. The Yamamoto mission, thrown together at the last minute, would be no exception. As McLanahan, in No. 116 ("Lady Luck") taxied onto the Marston matting a tire caught a sharp edge of the steel mat and blew out, leaving him stranded.

Mitchell continued circling slowly to allow Kittel, leading the remaining planes of the top cover flight, to catch up. When the last man was airborne and

US pilots cluster for a briefing, Guadalcanal. John Mitchell's final operational instructions to the pilots he had selected for the Yamamoto mission would have taken place in a similarly informal but professional environment. "On the eve of the flight, the mission was thoroughly explained to each pilot – there were no generalities," the official mission report states. "Each minute detail was discussed, with nothing taken for granted." (Alamy)

The Lightning Rex Barber borrowed from Bob Petit for the Yamamoto mission, P-38 No. 147 ("Miss Virginia") returned to Guadalcanal severely shot up but still in a flightworthy state. However, even after being patched together it lasted for little more than another month before a belly-landing which reduced it to the condition captured in this photo and left no other option than to scrap it. (NARA)

in formation, Mitchell began a slow descent toward the water on a heading of 265 degrees. It was now 0725.

As each pilot settled into position, they switched fuel selectors from internal fuel to the belly tanks. After a few seconds, Joe Moore's engines coughed and he quickly switched back to the mains. He tried again but the belly tanks would not feed. Disappointed, he pulled up beside Lanphier and hand-signaled that he would have to return to Fighter Two.

The attack section had been halved even before leaving US airspace. Fortunately, Mitchell had anticipated just such an exigency. He signaled the two spare element pilots to join Lanphier and Barber.

We were of course on complete radio silence – this was briefed the night before that no one was to touch that button on the way up there from takeoff until after the mission was completed. So without any words at all being spoken on the radio, we got Holmes into the right position, we got Hine in the right position, and we were on our way.

The P-38s followed Mitchell's descent down to 50ft. Flying this low to avoid detection, "I had nothing to do on the flight up," Canning recollected; "we were spread out and so I started counting sharks. I counted forty-eight sharks on the way up there. I saw a pod of whales and a huge manta ray about ten feet across, and I thought it was very interesting." Mitchell confirmed "it was kind of a dull flight, really … nothing happened on the way up." The greatest threat to the mission was environmental, for "it was hot, hot as hell in those cockpits." Built as a high-altitude escort fighter, the P-38 canopy could not open in flight to regulate the cockpit temperature. Instead, it acted as a convection oven, building up heat as the sun beat down on it. With nothing but the somnolent roll of the waves in their field of vision for two hours, the pilots were in real danger of dozing off.

Mitchell remained focused on the compass, and checked his watch frequently. After flying on a heading of 265 degrees on the first and longest leg for 55 minutes, he turned 25 degrees right to 290 degrees. Twenty-seven minutes later, he turned to 305 degrees. This leg was flown for 38 minutes; then to 20 degrees for the 40-mile leg to the south edge of Empress Bay, toward the coast. As he crossed the bay, he turned to 90 degrees. With the flight now approximately four minutes from the calculated interception point "I tried to close the squadron in because I wanted them where I could see them. We'd spread out quite a bit, so everyone closed in when I rocked my wings and we had a fairly tight formation going in." Flying east – into the sun – Mitchell could not

make out the coast, and "this concerned me very much," as he feared having miscalculated his approach. But then, out of the haze, "I saw a beach and there we were just about where I wanted us to be off the southwest corner of Bougainville." In an extraordinary act of navigation, the flight had arrived at the precise location intended and, at 0934, only one minute ahead of the scheduled time. And right on top of them, passing serenely overhead, was the anticipated flight of Japanese aircraft. Everything appeared to be falling into place. As the official after-action report later noted, "It was almost as if the affair had been pre-arranged with the mutual consent of friend and foe."

Yamamoto's last flight

Blissfully ignorant about the hubbub of activity on Guadalcanal, Japanese preparations on Rabaul had proceeded as planned. Although not aware their codes had been compromised, many of Yamamoto's peers harbored deep misgivings about the entire venture. "If he insists on going, six fighters are nothing like enough," Ozawa Jisaburo, C-in-C of the Third Fleet, fretted to senior staff officer Kuroshima. "Tell the chief of staff that he can have as many of my planes as he likes." But Ugaki was in bed with dengue fever, and Ozawa's proposal never reached him.

On the 17th, Yamamoto had lunch with Lieutenant General Hitoshi Imamura, commander of the ground forces at Rabaul. Two months earlier, on February 10, Imamura had hitched a ride with a navy plane to Buin on a visit to officers and men under his command. Ten minutes before they were due to land they were ambushed by a flight of American fighters, only escaping by seeking cover in the clouds. By relating this experience Imamura had hoped to impress Yamamoto with the dangers involved in flying to the front lines, but the Admiral merely expressed satisfaction at Imamura's

P-38s in flight over Guadalcanal. The standard single 165-gallon external fuel tank is clearly evidenced. This had proved sufficient for standard operations to date, but for the Yamamoto mission had to be supplemented with an additional 310-gallon drop tank. Navy planning for the Yamamoto mission had originally focused on interdicting the Admiral on the open water after he boarded a subchaser from Ballale Island to Bougainville. Army Major Mitchell's insistence on taking out Yamamoto's bomber in the air proved fortuitous, for Yamamoto was not in fact en route to Ballale but was flying directly to Buin airfield on Bougainville. Had the mission proceeded with the original plan, the US fighters would have missed Yamamoto altogether. (NARA)

Immaculate in his dress white uniform, Yamamoto offers encouragement to his pilots during Operation *I-Go*, Rabaul, 1943. Yamamoto had switched to a field uniform for the fateful trip of April 18, 1943, but his body was found still clutching the ceremonial sword he bears here. Standing directly to the Admiral's left is his Chief of Staff, Matome Ugaki. He survived the events of April 18, 1943, but never forgave himself for doing so. On August 15, 1945, the day of Japan's surrender, Ugaki, who was then C-in-C of the Fifth Air Fleet, led 11 of the Suisei carrier-based bombers under his command in a final suicide raid against Okinawa. At his side he wore a short sword that had been given to him by Yamamoto. (Alamy)

escape and the skill shown by his pilot, and showed no sign of being deterred.

On the night of April 17, Rear Admiral Takoji Joshima, C-in-C of the 11th Air Flotilla on Shortland and a long-time friend of Yamamoto, was horrified when he saw the radio message dispatched four days earlier. "What a damn fool thing to do, to send such a long and detailed message about the activities of the C. in C. so near the front! This kind of thing must stop." Joshima flew in to Rabaul and warned Yamamoto personally that he should abort the planned inspection, labeling it "an open invitation to the enemy" because of the proximity to American airbases. But Yamamoto refused to be dissuaded. "I have to go," he said. "I've let them know, and they'll have got things ready for me. I'll leave tomorrow morning and be back by dusk. Why don't we have dinner together?"

For security reasons, the pilots and crews of the two bombers selected for the mission were not informed of their roles until after the lights were turned off at 2100 that evening. At dawn on April 18, just as the American fighters

JAPANESE PERSONNEL

205th Kokutai, IJNAF

G4M "Betty" Bomber No. 323

7 Crew: Pilot, copilot, observer, 2 radio operators, gunner and mechanic

4 Passengers:
Adm. Isoroku Yamamoto, C-in-C, Combined Fleet
R.Adm. Rokuro Takada, Chief Surgeon, Combined Fleet
Cdr. Noburu Fukasaki, Yamamoto aide
Cdr. Kurio Toibana, Staff Officer

G4M "Betty" bomber No. 326

7 Crew: Pilot, copilot, observer, 2 radio operators, gunner and mechanic

5 Passengers:
V.Adm. Matome Ugaki, Chief of Staff, Combined Fleet
Capt. Motoharu Kitamura, Chief Paymaster, Combined Fleet
Cdr. Rinji Tomoro, Meteorology Officer, Combined Fleet
Cdr. Kaoni Imananka, Staff Officer
Cdr. Suteji Muroi, Staff Officer

204th Kokutai, IJNAF

6 A6M "Zero" pilots:
Chief Petty Officer Yoshimi Hidaka
Lt. Takeshi Morizaki
Petty Officer 2cl Yasuji Okazaki
Flt. Petty Officer Shoichi Sugita
Flt. Petty Officer Toyomitsu Tsujinoue
Flt. Petty Officer Kenji Yanagiya

passed over the Russell Islands on the first leg of their mission, two Type-1 Betty bombers of the 705th Squadron took off from Vunakanau airfield in the hills of Rabaul and flew the seven miles to Lakunai airfield, on New Britain's east coast. The pilots switched off their engines to wait, and before long Yamamoto and his entourage arrived.

Yamamoto was wearing field green, having decided it would be inappropriate to arrive at the front line in his dress white uniform. He did retain his white gloves and a dress sword. After saying goodbye to Vice Admiral Ozawa and the others who had come to see him off, four passengers – Yamamoto, Fleet Medical Officer Takada, Air "A" Staff Officer Toibana, and an aide, Fukusaki – boarded the first plane, No. 323, with Chief Petty Officer Kotani captain and chief pilot. Chief of Staff Ugaki, Fleet Paymaster Kitamura, Fleet Meteorological Officer Tomoro, Communications Staff Officer Imananka, and Air "B" Staff Officer Muroi boarded the second plane, No. 326, with Petty Officer First Class Tanimoto captain and Petty Officer Second Class Hayashi chief pilot. The flight crew were all highly experienced, reliable men, veterans of many battles. The weather was fine and visibility good – a pleasant day for flying.

The two bombers took off at 0600hrs, precisely on schedule, and were joined by the six escorting Zero fighters from No. 204 Kaigun Kokutai. As a concession to security, and to permit the Combined Fleet commander to see something of his deployed forces, the flight path made its first landfall at the southern tip of New Ireland, then turned south along the east coast of Bougainville, past the Japanese bases at Buka and Kieta, then on to Buin.

The Zeros formed up in two flights of three, each in a "V" formation. The Japanese kept the mountains of Bougainville to their left on the assumption that if they were to encounter American fighters these would have to come from the seaward side. The bombers maintained an altitude of 6,500ft with the fighters at 8,200ft above and a mile behind on either side of them.

A Japanese Navy G4M (Betty) Bomber skims the waves while under attack by a PB4Y-1 Patrol Bomber of US Navy Squadron 106 (VB-106), in the South Pacific area, 1943–44. Ugaki's Betty would have presented a similar profile as it fled the American intruders over Bougainville. (Naval History and Heritage Command)

Ugaki's Betty carried its regular armament of three 13mm guns and one 20mm gun, but because of the weight of the ammunition boxes, the squadron leader ordered only one belt for each weapon. There is no evidence Yamamoto's Betty was armed at all. As the Japanese held air superiority at Buin, they did not anticipate enemy action. There was no preflight briefing given to any of the flight crew about the location of enemy bases or the possibility of encountering American interceptors during the flight. In addition, the escort pilots had stripped the radios from their fighters to save weight. This meant they would be unable to communicate with the bombers. At every level, Japanese operational security was incredibly lax. At 0605hrs, the base commander at Rabaul east airfield sent a message informing the base commander at Ballale of the departure of two land-based attack planes and six Zero fighters. Another message was sent after takeoff by the chief pilot of the plane carrying Yamamoto, informing Ballale base that they were "due to arrive 0745." Both messages were sent in simple flight codes, though even an immediate decryption would not have allowed the necessary time to prepare an attack.

Ugaki recorded his plane

> was flying in excellent formation to the left and slightly to the rear of Yamamoto's aircraft – so excellent that at times the wingtips seemed almost in danger of touching, and I could clearly see the profile of the C. in C., sitting in the captain's seat, and the forms of people moving about inside the plane. It was a comfortable flight as I sat listening to explanations, with reference to flight maps, of objects visible on the ground below.

Before long, Ugaki, who was sitting in the captain's seat immediately behind chief pilot Hayashi, nodded off. At 0730 the flight caught its first glimpse of Ballale and began a shallow descent in preparation for landing. Tanimoto, who was in the copilot's seat, passed the still half-asleep Ugaki a note that read: "Expect to arrive at Ballale 0745." The formation was flying along the west coast of Bougainville, with dense jungle visible below.

Suddenly, one of the escort fighters accelerated ahead of the second bomber. It dipped its wings, and the pilot could be seen pointing to something. Another of the escort Zeros approached the lead bomber, which promptly increased speed and pushed its nose down in a rapid descent. At the controls of the second bomber was Hiroshi Hayashi, a flight petty officer second class in the Japanese Navy assigned to the 705th Air Squadron, who had served for nearly a year at Rabaul. His immediate response was professional indignation; it was dangerous to drop altitude at such a rate. But his ordeal was just beginning.

The interception

It was Doug Canning, flying No. 3 in the flight, who broke radio silence: "Bogeys! Eleven o'clock high!" At that moment, Mitchell spotted not one but two Japanese bombers crossing the western tip of Bougainville 5 miles away at about 4,500ft in a shallow descent toward Ballale with six Zeros behind them in two flights of three about a thousand feet higher. He replied "Roger," and "I have 'em."

A factory model P-38 undergoing trials somewhere over open water. The long, level flight from Guadalcanal to Bougainville was in some ways the most challenging aspect of the Yamamoto mission. Because there was no immediate threat, the pilots had trouble concentrating and were at risk of veering off course or straight down into the Pacific. "People ask, 'What were you thinking about on the way up there?'" John Mitchell later noted. "I was thinking, 'Am I going to be on time? God, it's hot in here,' and things like that, and actually nothing happened on the way up." Doug Canning kept his mind active by cataloging the marine wildlife he encountered. (NARA)

The P-38s were still at wave-top height and heading toward the Japanese aircraft at a 90-degree angle. Mitchell turned right, parallel with their track, and firewalled his engine to climb as fast as he could. He ordered his pilots to "skin off your tanks" and pulled his own belly tank release, watching as Jacobson, Canning, and Goerke dropped theirs.

Holmes' tanks wouldn't detach: "I jiggled the release, I checked the circuit breakers, nothing happened. I couldn't drop them." He radioed the killer flight leader, "Wait a minute, Tom, I'll tear my tanks off, just give me a second." Getting no response from Lanphier, Holmes pulled away from the formation back out over the water, turning seaward and nosing down to pick up speed, hoping the acceleration would help shake the tanks loose. "That was a mistake as far as I was concerned," Mitchell later noted, while showing due deference to Hine, Holmes' wingman, who "rightfully followed him to protect him."

TWO: ENGAGEMENT TO DOWNING

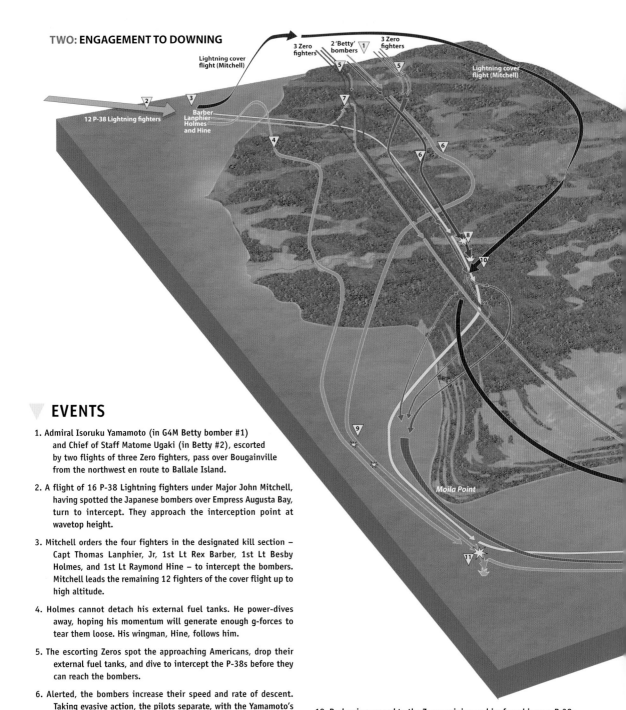

Lightning cover flight (Mitchell)

3 Zero fighters

2 'Betty' bombers

3 Zero fighters

Lightning cover flight (Mitchell)

12 P-38 Lightning fighters

Barber Lanphier Holmes and Hine

Moila Point

EVENTS

1. Admiral Isoruku Yamamoto (in G4M Betty bomber #1) and Chief of Staff Matome Ugaki (in Betty #2), escorted by two flights of three Zero fighters, pass over Bougainville from the northwest en route to Ballale Island.

2. A flight of 16 P-38 Lightning fighters under Major John Mitchell, having spotted the Japanese bombers over Empress Augusta Bay, turn to intercept. They approach the interception point at wavetop height.

3. Mitchell orders the four fighters in the designated kill section – Capt Thomas Lanphier, Jr, 1st Lt Rex Barber, 1st Lt Besby Holmes, and 1st Lt Raymond Hine – to intercept the bombers. Mitchell leads the remaining 12 fighters of the cover flight up to high altitude.

4. Holmes cannot detach his external fuel tanks. He power-dives away, hoping his momentum will generate enough g-forces to tear them loose. His wingman, Hine, follows him.

5. The escorting Zeros spot the approaching Americans, drop their external fuel tanks, and dive to intercept the P-38s before they can reach the bombers.

6. Alerted, the bombers increase their speed and rate of descent. Taking evasive action, the pilots separate, with the Yamamoto's #1 Betty banking to the right, and #2 Betty to the left.

7. Lanphier banks up and into the three Zeros diving at him, scattering them. They regroup and pursue him.

8. Ignoring the three Zeros on his six, Barber latches onto the tail of Yamamoto's #1 Betty and shoots it down.

9. Holmes finally shakes off his external fuel tanks. He and Hine turn back toward the action and single out #2 Betty, both of them pouring fire into the Japanese aircraft.

10. Barber is exposed to the Zeros gaining on him from his rear. P-38s from the cover flight dive and scatter the Japanese fighters.

11. Barber picks up the #2 Betty and joins the pursuit. His fire finishes off the Japanese aircraft, which crashes into the water off Moila Point.

12. With their mission accomplished, all American fighters break off and head individually back to base, pursued by the Zeros. Hine becomes separated and lost, presumably KIA. Every other Lightning makes it back home to Guadalcanal.

INTERCEPTING YAMAMOTO, BOUGAINVILLE, APRIL 18, 1943

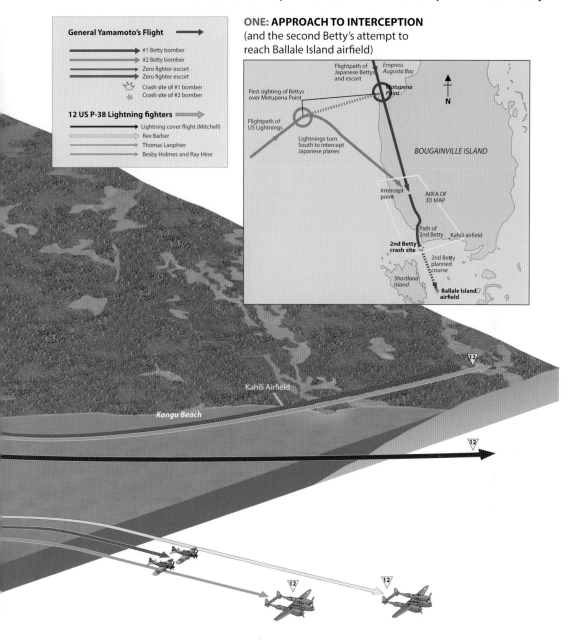

General Yamamoto's Flight ➤

- ➤ #1 Betty bomber
- ➤ #2 Betty bomber
- ➤ Zero fighter escort
- ➤ Zero fighter escort
- 🦶 Crash site of #1 bomber
- 🦶 Crash site of #2 bomber

12 US P-38 Lightning fighters ➤

- ➤ Lightning cover flight (Mitchell)
- ➤ Rex Barber
- ➤ Thomas Lanphier
- ➤ Besby Holmes and Ray Hine

ONE: APPROACH TO INTERCEPTION
(and the second Betty's attempt to reach Ballale Island airfield)

Empress Augusta Bay

Flightpath of Japanese Bettys and escort

Motupena Point

First sighting of Bettys over Motupena Point

Flightpath of US Lightnings

Lightnings turn South to intercept Japanese planes

N

BOUGAINVILLE ISLAND

Intercept point

AREA OF 3D MAP

Path of 2nd Betty

Kahili airfield

2nd Betty crash site

2nd Betty planned course

Shortland Island

Ballale Island airfield

Kahili Airfield

Kangu Beach

12

12

12

12

Intelligence, ingenuity, and stellar navigation had brought the US fighters to the precise point of contact. But from that moment, the entire operation seemed to be falling to pieces. Mitchell felt his heart sink; he now had only half as many fighters as planned to pit against twice as many bombers as anticipated. Worse, he could not order his remaining pilots to concentrate on one of the Bettys as he had no idea which one was Yamamoto's.

There was no time to draft an alternative strategy, and Mitchell refused to improvise. With icy resolve, he remained committed to the original attack plan. Mitchell led the covering flight in its climb to the predetermined CAP altitude as he radioed to Lanphier: "He's your meat, Tom." Lanphier acknowledged, and the two remaining planes of the killer flight turned toward the eight enemy aircraft on a rising intercept course.

The covering flight continued climbing, parallel to the Japanese planes. Mitchell was very tempted to level off and join in the pursuit. "If I had known they weren't going to send any fighters up from Kahili to greet the admiral, I would have made the attack. I would have taken over, Lanphier or anyone else be damned. I would have gone in first." He had opted for the high cover role because he anticipated mixing it up with the Zeros scrambling from Kahili. But none of these so much as got off the ground while the interception was in progress – "a big disappointment to me and the rest of the cover flight."

The action would therefore focus on the killer flight. All subsequent accounts agree that Lanphier (on the left side of the attacking element) made a climbing turn to the left (north by northwest). In so doing, he had gone nose to nose with the three escort Zeros on the seaward side of the formation. Barber, again by all subsequent accounts, banked hard right. Mitchell, watching from above radioed, "Get the bombers … damn it all, the bombers!" Neither Barber nor Lanphier would later recall hearing this radio transmission. They were too mission-focused.

At this point, the accounts diverge. Exactly what happened over the next few minutes has been the source of bitter contention for more than three-quarters of a century. The participants all went to their graves each swearing their perspective was the legitimate one, and no version of the story is compatible with any of the others.

From the Japanese point of view, the events of that day were perfectly straightforward. They were ambushed and defeated. The pilots in the escorting Zeros were caught completely by surprise and reacted fatally late to the threat. They were flying above the bombers and scanning the horizon ahead of them to the south; they never suspected American fighters would approach from behind them at a lower altitude. One of their number, Kenji Yanagiya, only realized they were under attack when the flight leader suddenly rocked his wings and went immediately into a full-throttle dive.

The immediate thought that went through his mind was not to try and shoot down the P-38s, but rather to deflect them from their attack path. All six of the Zeros made a straight dive from their higher altitude to position themselves between the bombers and the oncoming P-38s. Rather than firing at the American fighters, they kept shooting in front of the P-38s, trying to prevent them from closing on the Bettys. The enemy was relentless, however: "They were all firing at the bomber and they were just going in rows, so to speak. They were all firing ... Shoot, flip, go down – just like that."

Aboard the bombers, confusion was total. "What happened?" Ugaki called out to his plane's captain, who replied "It must be some mistake." The crew onboard took up battle stations, cleared their guns, and prepared for firing. "For a moment, the wind blowing in and the handling of machine guns and all caused one mixed, disturbing noise," Ugaki recalled. His bomber made a sudden evasive turn of more than 90 degrees. Having spotted the American fighters, the bomber's captain, "seeing an enemy plane about to make a dive at us, tapped the shoulder of the chief pilot, directing him to turn left or right." Yamamoto's and Ugaki's aircraft separated as they accelerated into their dives, the distance between them increasing as the No. 1 plane banked to the right, south-southwest toward the shoreline while the No. 2 plane banked east to the left.

As Ugaki's plane separated from the lead bomber he lost track of Yamamoto before finally locating the C-in-C's Betty. He was horrified to see the airplane, now skimming the jungle top, belching smoke and losing speed as it headed south. Ugaki ordered air staff officer Muroi, who was standing in the gangway diagonally behind him, to keep an eye on the C-in-C's plane, then turned to the pilot, shouting, "Follow plane No. 1! Follow plane No. 1!"

Hayashi, who was performing desperate escape maneuvers, sometimes using only his feet and sometimes only his hands as he banked the plane

The second Betty (overleaf)

While Ugaki remained fixated on the funeral pyre of the crashed bomber, his own plane straightened out from its frantic maneuvering and at full throttle raced out over the open sea toward Moila Point. Those onboard noticed the concentration of dogfighting planes in the area where Yamamoto's bomber had plunged into the jungle; but now, fighters were breaking from that group and turning toward them. Ugaki "stared hopelessly as a silver H-shaped P-38 half-rolled in a screaming zoom, then turned steeply, and closed rapidly toward our plane. Our gunners were firing desperately at the big enemy fighter, but to no avail."

Ugaki could only watch, helplessly, as:

the P-38's nose seemed to burst into twinkling flame, and suddenly the bomber shook from the impact of the enemy's machine gun bullets and cannon shells. The P-38 pilot was an excellent gunner, for his first fusillade of bullets and shells crashed into the right side of the airplane, then into the left. The drumming sounds vibrated through the airplane which rocked from the impact of the enemy fire. We knew we were now completely helpless, and waited for our end to come. The P-38 hung grimly to our tail, pouring in his deadly fire.

One by one, the answering 7.7mm machine guns onboard the Betty fell silent.

Abruptly our crew chief, who had been shouting orders to his men, fell from our view. Several of the crew were already dead, as the bullets screamed through the airplane. Commander Muroi sprawled over the chair and table in the fuselage compartment, his hands thrown out before him, his head rolling lifelessly back and forth as the plane shuddered.

Another cannon shell suddenly tore open the right wing. Hayashi brought his plane down until the propellers were in danger of hitting the water. Suddenly, he felt a shock and his controls went dead. His elevator had been shot away. With no guidance, the plane plunged straight down into the sea. It must have tilted quite sharply as it hit the water, for he saw one of the engines fly off at an angle.

For Ugaki, "everything turned black. I felt the crushing force of salt water pouring into the fuselage and almost immediately we were below the surface." Hayashi, too, momentarily lost consciousness. When he came to, he found himself in the water by the base of the left wing of the plane, which was on fire, lying half on its side with the tail and right wing sticking up high out of the sea.

Both men had been thrown clear of the wreckage off Moila Point at the southwestern extremity of Bougainville Island. Both started swimming for the shore, Ugaki clinging to floating debris. After coming under friendly fire from jumpy Army sentries, both were helped ashore and treated to first aid. Ugaki's injuries were severe, including a severed radial artery and compound fracture of the right arm. The only other survivor of the crash, Captain Kitamura, was rescued by a navy seaplane.

and put it into sharp turns, had also lost sight of the other bomber. "Tracers flashed by our wings, and the pilot frantically maneuvered to evade the pursuing fighter plane," Ugaki recalled. "I waited impatiently for the airplane to return to horizontal position, so that I could observe the admiral's bomber. Although I hoped for the best, I knew only too well what the fate of the airplane would be." His premonition was correct. Yamamoto's plane was no longer in sight; dominating the horizon was a column of black smoke boiling from the dense jungle into the air. His despair in that moment suffuses his diary entry: "Alas! It is all over!"

It is a matter of historical record, therefore, that *what* happened in the skies above Bougainville on the morning of April 18, 1943, is not in doubt. The question that remains, however, is *how* exactly it happened. The three surviving members of the kill flight all subsequently either published their own accounts or expressed their perspectives in interviews and public forums. They are impossible to harmonize.

The pilots' accounts

Tom Lanphier

In Lanphier's version, which was serialized in *The New York Times* from September 12 to 14, 1945, he and Barber had arrived at a point 2 miles to Yamamoto's right and about a mile in front of him before they were spotted by his Zero cover. The two Americans "saw their belly tanks drop – a sign that they were clearing for action – and they nosed over in a group to dive on us;" first the three Zeros which had been flying the seaward side of the bombers, then the three Zeros from the inshore side of the formation.

Instinctively, Lanphier swung his aircraft upward to bring his guns to bear and meet the diving Zeros head on. The lead enemy fighter opened fire first, but "He was a worse shot than I was, and he died. My machine guns and cannon ripped one of his wings away. He twisted under me, all flame and smoke. His two wingmen hurtled past and I wasted a few bursts between them," before twisting away to find the Bettys. "I kicked my ship over on its back and looked down for the lead Japanese bomber." He found it skimming the jungle, headed for Kahili. As he dived in pursuit, Lanphier could make out "a swirl of aircraft against the blue – a single Lightning silhouetted against the light in a swarm of Zeros. That was Barber, having himself a time."

Fearing he might have picked up too much speed in his dive, which would result in his overshooting the Betty, Lanphier cut back his throttles, crossing his controls and going into a skid in order to manage his descent. The two surviving Zeros from the trio he had tangled with earlier were now converging on him from an angle slightly off to his right, seeking to cut him off

Tom Lanphier, posing in front of a P-38 at Randolph Field, Texas, September 6, 1943 after being rotated back to the US from the South Pacific. Born in Panama, the Stanford University-educated Lanphier was raised in a military environment, and could claim none other than Jimmy Doolittle as his godfather. His father, Lt. Col. Thomas G. Lanphier, Sr., was a West Point graduate who had commanded the 1st Pursuit Group after WWI and was chief of the Air Unit, Intelligence Group, of the Military Intelligence Service, G-2, at Headquarters United States Army in Washington, DC during WWII. (NARA)

from the bomber. "The next three or four seconds spelled life or death," as Lanphier held his course, determined to make the most of "the one good shot I had coming up. I fired a long steady burst across the bomber's course of flight, from approximately right angles. The bomber's right engine, then its right wing, burst into flame. I had accomplished my part of the mission," as moments later, "the bomber's wing tore off. The bomber plunged into the jungle. It exploded. That was the end of Admiral Isoroku Yamamoto."

A later account expands on the moment of the kill. Diving at the bomber from astern, Lanphier leveled out, dropping his flaps and skidding to slow down.

> I cleared the guns at him, and when I did, the right engine started to burn. I was at about 70 degrees to the bomber, which is an impossible angle to hit anything, but I kept on my curve of pursuit and his right wing began to burn also. Just as I went behind him, with his cannon shooting out the rear end, the wing came off and he bellywhopped into the jungle and I went on past.

Lanphier was not out of the woods yet. The two Zeros were making another pass at him, almost at right angles to his left. He radioed Mitchell for assistance at getting the vengeful Japanese fighters off his back. Hugging the ground, Lanphier traversed the airfield at Kahili, made the harbor, and headed east. This accounts for the references some P-38 pilots would make to engaging Japanese fighters scrambling from Kahili airfield. In fact, none of these got in the air until after the Americans had dispersed for home; the Zeros they encountered were the ones from the escort mission who had broken off their pursuit of Lanphier.

As Lanphier climbed and accelerated away from Bougainville he could reflect on the fact "I was away with only two bullet holes in my rudder. Nothing more, except a year or two off my life."

In addition to his account in *The New York Times*, a bylined article by Lanphier was distributed by the North American Newspaper Alliance (NANA) in 1945. This included two specific references to confirmation of the kills. In his account, after radioing Mitchell for assistance in shaking off the pursuing Zeros, he then asked his flight leader "to verify the burning bomber. He replied that he could see it."

In reality, while maintaining cover at 18,000ft, Mitchell could hear a lot of chatter on the radio but was otherwise isolated from the fight.

> I looked down and saw some black smoke coming out of the jungle. Lanphier said something about a plane going down and did I see it? I told him I saw a pillar of smoke coming out of the jungle but I had no way of knowing if it was a Betty, a Zero, or a P-38. I saw none of the action below.

Lanphier also stated he saw three columns of black smoke rising out of the jungle behind him, which were "the burning bomber containing Yamamoto and two of his accompanying aircraft." Lanphier assigned exclusive credit for bringing down the second Betty to Barber:

When I had pulled up into the Zeros on our first contact with the enemy, Rex had bored on in after the bomber coming our way. Ignoring the other three Zeros, who were by no means ignoring him, he opened fire on his target. The bomber passed under his right wing, still apparently undamaged. Despite the fact that he was now the concerted target of all three escorting Zeros, he bulled his way back through their fire and latched onto the bomber once again. This time he drove his attack perfectly home blasting off the entire tail section of the Mitsubishi, which rolled over on its back and plummeted to the earth far below. No one jumped out of it.

Besby Holmes

A second perspective on the events of April 18 was offered by Holmes, beginning with him still trying to detach his external fuel tanks. Having reached approximately 350mph in his dive, he hauled back on the stick and kicked hard the left rudder. The tanks tore off, and he looked back to see what was happening. He could hear someone – he believed it was Lanphier – yelling, "I'm bracketed by three Zeros and can't go anywhere but straight ahead!"

Just then he heard Barber shout, "I got one of the sons of bitches! His tail fell off!" and saw a bomber drop into the jungle and explode "with a terrific flash … a tight ball of fire, as though it had gone almost straight in." He then spotted a P-38 chasing a Betty, and in turn being chased by three Zeros. He and Hine barrel-rolled down to assist the Lightning pilot, "who was in a predicament." At that moment, given he had just radioed for assistance, "I thought it was Lanphier. It turned out to be Rex Barber, but at that point I didn't know and I didn't care." In fact, "Lanphier wasn't in sight. I was told later that he was chased to the vicinity of Kahili airfield by three Zeros and finally lost them in a cloud of dust being kicked up by the swarm of Zeros scrambling for takeoff to help save Yamamoto. I did not see Lanphier in the fight after that initial attack."

Instructing Hine to take the Zero on Barber's right wing, Holmes slid over to target the two crowding him from the left. "As I slipped in behind the first Zero, I saw the Betty bomber fleeing in front of Barber's P-38. What a beautiful, easy target, I thought. We had to get that bomber if it was the last thing we ever did, but first we had to knock the three Zeros off Barber's back." Holmes destroyed one Zero, which "exploded in a sheet of flame." The other Japanese pilot "was evidently so intent upon getting Barber that he either didn't see me or was too stubborn to break off the fight." Seconds after Holmes opened fire, the second Zero "flamed and fell off into an inverted dive into the sea." Given the low altitude, the pilot of this Zero "could not have survived even if he weren't on fire."

With his airspeed indicating 425mph, Holmes zoomed past Barber just as Hine shot down the last Zero on Barber's right wing. The frantic Betty was now flying straight ahead, "a sitting duck as far as I was concerned." Holmes pulled up even with it, setting up a high side gunnery pass: "I chose that method of attack rather than go directly at the tail, which contained a couple of deadly heavy caliber stingers. By this time the Japanese gunners on the bomber were all firing at me."

As Holmes closed in on the Betty, which was now flying barely above the water, "I fired a short burst of my fifties to get the proper deflection and check the range. There was no need to be in a hurry. There was still sufficient time to shoot the bomber down in my own way. The next burst of fifties kicked up the water just short of the bomber."

Having established the range, Holmes opened fire with his .50cal guns. Bullets tore into the Betty, and Holmes opened up with his 20mm cannon. The gunners who had been sniping at him from the Betty stopped firing. Now he could slide in directly behind for a stern shot. The Betty was now no more than 10 miles from Kahili, and Holmes could see clouds of dust rising from the Zeros scrambling for takeoff.

Flying in extremely close, Holmes lined up the bomber's right engine and touched the triggers. The bullets tore into the engine and wing root and he could see little tongues of flame leap out. Holmes could hear himself yelling, "Go down! Go down! Go down or blow up, dammit!" He continued to squeeze the triggers and sent a long burst into the engine. A huge puff of smoke, followed by orange flame, burst from the engine cowling. As the bomber stalled, Holmes rammed the stick forward to pass under it; "I saw the shadow of the bomber over me, and immediately hauled back sharply on the controls to keep from crashing into the water." As he pulled up to make another pass, he saw the Betty crash,

> hit the water with great force, break into pieces, perhaps the last quarter to the last third of the tail section came up and rotated backward and smashed right into the middle of a burning funeral pyre, and that's about the time Rex Barber went through it, and that's how he got all the shrapnel in the leading edge of his wing.

As the three American fighters headed toward the open sea Holmes spotted a Zero, outbound from Kahili, on Barber's tail. He flipped over, forced the Japanese fighter to break off and, with his 20mm guns dry, caught it with his remaining .50cal: "I saw a burst of flame from the Zero as he went out of control."

Taking stock of the situation, Holmes found himself alone, but "I was still alive and had saved Barber's neck for the second time that day. I had also added another Zero to my list of kills, making my total for the day one bomber and three Zeros."

Rex Barber

Finally, we have Barber's account. He and Lanphier were approaching the bombers from approximately 90 degrees and still climbing to get to an altitude at least level with the two bombers when suddenly the Bettys increased their rate of descent markedly. Evidently, the American fighters had been sighted, for the three Zeros, above and lagging a considerable distance to the right behind the Bettys, nosed over in a steep dive and jettisoned their external fuel tanks, followed moments later by the other three Zeros on the left side.

Rex Barber in full flight gear, complete with "Mae West" life vest. Barber arrived at Guadalcanal with the 70th Pursuit Squadron in December 1942. Flying a Bell P-39 Airacobra, he scored his first victory by downing a Japanese bomber on the 28th. He began flying P-38 Lightnings when he transferred to the 339th Fighter Squadron (FS). (Matt Simek)

It was apparent the three Zeros closest to the Bettys on the right side would catch up with the bombers at the same time as the P-38s would break right to turn in on their firing pass, meaning the American fighters would be a perfect target for the bomber's escorts.

Just before that could happen, Lanphier suddenly broke about 90 degrees to the left and started a head-on pass up and into the oncoming Zeros. "This was a wise maneuver on his part as it allowed me the opportunity to attack the bombers without the Zeros on my tail," Barber noted. By single-handedly taking on the escorts, Lanphier had cleared a path for Barber to complete the mission. He banked sharply right to fall in behind the Bettys. In so doing, his left engine and wing briefly blocked out his view of both bombers. As he rolled back, there was only one Betty in front of him; he didn't know if it was the lead bomber or not.

By this time they were no more than 1,000ft above the jungle canopy, and the Betty again increased its dive in an attempt to get to treetop level. Barber's turn had carried him slightly to the left of the Betty and he had closed to approximately 50 yards behind it. He opened fire, aiming over the fuselage at the right engine. The bomber was shuddering at each burst, and Barber could see chunks of its engine cowling detaching. As he slid over to get directly behind the target, his line of fire passed through the vertical fin of the Betty. Some pieces of the rudder separated. As he moved right, he continued firing into the right engine, which began to emit heavy, black smoke from around the cowling. Continuing to rake the bomber with his guns, Barber shifted his fire back along the wing root and into the fuselage, then on into the left engine. All the while, "I got no fire back from the bomber at all," strongly implying it was not armed for the flight.

Barber was now no more than 100ft behind the bomber and almost level with it when the Betty suddenly "almost stopped in mid-air … His right wing came up very violently." The Betty made a quarter snap to its left, "the kind of a stall that would come from the pilot being killed and involuntarily yanking back on the controls." Barber almost collided with the doomed bomber's right wing; his last visual of the Betty as he roared by was over his left shoulder, where he saw the bomber "with its wing upended vertically and black smoke pouring from the right engine. I believe the Betty crashed into the jungle, although I did not see it crash."

Meanwhile, the second flight of three Zeros had caught up and were making firing passes at him. Barber turned to the right and headed toward the coast at treetop level while taking violent evasive action. Unwittingly, by calling for assistance, Lanphier had saved Barber a second time. Responding to the appeal, Mitchell and his wingman Jacobson, followed by Canning and his wingman Goerke, dived into the melee coming to Lanphier's rescue. At top speed, Mitchell and Jacobson latched on to a Zero and both fired a few shots but without registering any hits. This corresponds to Barber's account. After shooting down Yamamoto's Betty, he found himself struggling to shrug off the escorting Zeros. Suddenly, "two P-38s made a head-on pass at me; they were coming at very high speed and down, and they shot over me and into the Zeros that were behind me. The Zeros broke and scattered."

When Barber looked inland and to his rear, he saw a large column of black smoke rising from the jungle, "which I believed to be the Betty I had shot down." As he headed toward the coast, he saw Holmes and Hine in pursuit of a Betty just offshore, heading south. The Betty was so low that its propellers were making wakes in the water.

Holmes started firing, walking his rounds up and through the right engine, which began trailing a white vapor. Hine started to fire, but he was too tight on Holmes' right wing; the two fighters "were flying much too close a formation for any accurate gunnery pattern," and all his rounds hit well ahead in the water. Holmes and Hine passed over the Betty and headed south while Barber dropped in behind it, closing to less than 50 yards. He opened fire, aiming at the right engine. In his words, "I fired one burst and the bomber disintegrated … He flew all to pieces." Barber later concluded Holmes' rounds "must have hit the tanks and filled [the bomber's] wings with gas fumes, because the ship exploded in my face." As he flew through the black smoke and debris, a large chunk of the Betty hit his right wing, cutting out his turbo supercharger intercooler. Another large piece hit the underside of his gondola, making a very large dent in it.

Up ahead, Holmes and Hine had encountered Zeros, which Barber assumed had taken off from the Kahili airstrip. Barber saw Hine heading east and out to sea, smoke trailing from his right engine, and a Zero explode under Holmes' guns. "There was another Zero coming in, but he was not looking at me, evidently he was looking at this disaster that had just happened to his friend,

Lieutenant Rex Barber (fifth from left) poses with the portside wing of P-38 No. 125 ("Diablo"), which he flew on the mission against a Japanese floatplane base in the Shortland Islands on March 29, 1943. The last four feet of the wingtip were left embedded in the radio mast of his target, Japanese subchaser No. 28, during a strafing. Another P-38, No. 138 ("Old Ironsides") was written off when it crash-landed upon returning from the same mission; its portside wing was cannibalized for No. 125, enabling Major Louis Kittel to pilot it during the Yamamoto mission. Captain Thomas Lanphier, section leader during the Shortlands mission, is seventh from the left in this photo. (Matt Simek)

and I managed a short burst into his fuselage and he also caught fire and crashed." Barber looked out over the water for signs of a crash and spotted three oil slicks, one where the Betty had gone in and one each where the Zeros he and Holmes shot down had crashed. Low on fuel, he turned for home.

At some point, Holmes lost touch with Hine. Given his account of the action, this is hardly surprising; as Mitchell put it, with unwonted sarcasm, "If Holmes did all the didos [trick maneuvers] that he said he did, I don't see how any wingman could have stayed with him."

After becoming separated, Hine may have fallen victim to Yanagiya. The Japanese pilot had elected to swoop low over Kahili airfield and fire a short burst with his machine guns, the emergency alert signal to scramble the available fighters. He then decided to head east in a bid to cut off the American fighters on their return path. Shortly after passing over Shortland Island, while flying at an altitude of 12,000ft, he spotted one P-38 flying 3,000ft below him. Firing from above and behind the Lightning, he saw vapor trailing out of one of its engines and observed that it was gradually losing altitude before losing track of it.

This is consistent with American accounts. Holmes reported seeing Hine's aircraft trailing smoke or vapor from the left engine and heading in the general direction of Wilson Strait, southwest of Shortland Island. Mitchell reported that Hine's left engine was hit and began to smoke, and he was last seen at 0940hrs, losing altitude 4 miles north of Shortland Island with three Zeros on his tail.

Mitchell received word the second Betty had gone down in the water, "so since we had gotten the two bombers, I started climbing and radioed, 'Mission accomplished. Everybody, get your ass home.'" Kittel, now leading the top cover of eight P-38s, replied with a simple "Roger." Disappointed at having had no action, he turned his flight toward Guadalcanal. Concerned about Hine, Mitchell made a couple of circles before departing, "looking for an oil slick or somebody floating around in a yellow Mae West. I didn't see anything." The last American out of the area was Canning, who was closing in on another Zero when his windshield misted over, causing him to lose his quarry. When his vision cleared he had lost contact with the rest of the flight: "there was not one soul there but me." Now the lone P-38 still over Bougainville, far below he could see "many, many Zeros" taking off from Kahili. Thinking to himself, "This is no place for Doug Canning to be," he gunned his engines and headed home. The first to spot Yamamoto's flight, he was the last to leave the combat area.

The skies over Buin, which had been torn by aircraft in a snarling dogfight, were now eerily quiet. Yanagiya recalled that the Buin airfield had always been noted for the great clouds of dust that swirled around when aircraft took off and landed. In order to get ready for the expected arrival of the C-in-C, the Buin airfield commander had ordered all hands to participate in a massive cleanup of the runway. Officers and men worked all night. When the Zeros came in to land, the pilots were surprised to see the base's entire garrison standing at attention in spotless dress uniforms along the freshly cleaned runway.

AFTERMATH

Homecoming

With the mission accomplished, the P-38 flight broke up as each pilot headed for home individually. All of them made it back to Guadalcanal, but one.

There is circumstantial evidence Hine may have at least temporarily escaped his pursuers. On the morning of April 18, a PBY Catalina of Navy Patrol Squadron 44 piloted by Lieutenant Harry Metke took off from Espíritu Santo bound for New Georgia to deliver supplies to coastwatchers and pick up a downed airman. As they neared the New Georgia coast the crew spotted over a dozen P-38s flying below them at wave-top level, heading toward Bougainville. After delivering its cargo, the PBY again took off to continue its patrol. The crew heard radio chatter over the intercom from the P-38 pilots, who were in a furious air battle.

Returning to Espíritu Santo, the PBY encountered a damaged P-38, its left engine stopped and the propeller feathered. Metke contacted the P-38 pilot via radio, asked if he was OK, and told him that if he wanted to ditch, the PBY could easily pick him up. After asking for a compass heading for Guadalcanal, the pilot replied he could make it back to base on one engine, and then flew off and out of sight.

If that pilot was Hine, then either he miscalculated the fuel-to-distance ratio, or the damage to his aircraft was more extensive than he appreciated. He and his P-38 were never found; COMAIRSOLS called off the search on May 28, 1943.

Operating at the limit of their range, the other pilots sweated out their return flights. After checking his fuel gauges, Holmes was immediately aware he could not make it back to Guadalcanal. From the standard cruising speed of 260mph he throttled back to 170mph, just enough power to keep his fighter from stalling, and set course for the newly constructed airfield on the Russell Islands. With Doug Canning alongside him, Holmes kept switching back and forth between his tanks to squeeze every last drop of gasoline into his fuel lines. Finally, the Russell Islands hove into view on the horizon. The airfield was still cluttered with steamrollers and other heavy construction equipment. Holmes urged Canning to drag the airstrip and scatter the crews. Holmes then set down hard. His Lightning came to a skidding halt near the far end of the track. When he opened the canopy his flying suit was soaked through.

Canning returned to Guadalcanal. Later that day, a Navy patrol torpedo boat arrived. Since these small craft were powered by the same Allison engines as the P-38, the captain generously allocated Holmes enough fuel for him to make it back to Guadalcanal a few hours later.

Meanwhile, Barber also returned to Guadalcanal, landing at Fighter Two "almost out of gas," he recalled. His crew chief then showed him the four bullet holes through the blades of his left propeller and the three in his right propeller. There were 104 in-and-out bullet holes in the wings, tail section, and fuselage, probably from 52 hits, all from the rear to front. "This confirmed for me that I was hit from behind by the Zeros, not by the gunners on the Bettys."

As they arrived, one by one, Mitscher met his pilots with a case of bourbon, Viccellio a case of fresh milk, both in their own right luxuries that signified how proud the commanders were of their men.

Their pride must have been tempered by the indiscipline of one flight member. "We weren't supposed to let the Japanese know in any way, shape, or form that we might have broken their code," top cover pilot Roger J. Ames notes. But Lanphier couldn't contain his enthusiasm, or his desire to stake the first claim. Still a few miles out from the island he called "Recon," the Guadalcanal fighter director station. When Lieutenant Edward C. Hutcheson, the officer on duty, responded, Lanphier yelled jubilantly – on an uncoded channel – "I got Yamamoto! I got the son-of-bitch! He won't dictate peace terms in the White House now!"

More than 40 years later, Ames painfully recalled about the return from the mission, "All I can remember is how upset I was when Tom Lanphier made his statement over the open mike."

Lanphier had lost none of his ebullient attitude once he touched down. Lieutenant Joseph O. Young recalled that Lanphier was the first to land. "From the aircraft he claimed victory over Admiral Yamamoto in no uncertain terms. His reaction was astounding to me and appeared to be irrational. He was visibly shaken, but very adamant about his victory."

Lanphier said later he wanted to make a pass and victory roll over Henderson and Fighter Two but with his fuel gauge reading empty, he knew he might not make it. He said his left engine quit on the landing roll and he came to a stop near the end of the runway. Ground crews ran out to his plane and swarmed around him as he climbed out of the cockpit. He kept repeating, "I got the son-of-a-bitch! I got Yamamoto!" Everybody patted him on the back as he unbuckled his parachute and got into a waiting jeep.

Lieutenant Bill Harris, a pilot who did not go on the mission, saw Lanphier coming down the runway in a jeep from where his airplane was parked and heard him call out several times, loudly, "I got him! I got him!

I got that son-of-a-bitch!" John Mitchell also recalled after he landed that he saw Lanphier coming down the taxiway in a jeep, "waving and hollering, 'I got Yamamoto!'"

Louis Kittel, leader of the eight top cover aircraft, said that when he parked his aircraft, his ground crew told him of the results of the mission. "Lanphier apparently announced to the flight crew that he had shot the big man down, because when I parked that was the word my crew conveyed to me."

Critically, in light of the controversy that subsequently metastasized, there was no formal debriefing of any of the returning pilots. The pilots were greeted by Pugh, Viccellio, Morrison, and Condon, to whom "they reported just the things we know from their statements." Condon noted: "What happened, what they saw and did on the mission. That was all. That was sent in and was put in the COMAIRSOLS' summary: who shot down so many bombers, so many fighters."

According to Brooklyn Harris, squadron clerk for the 339th who also acted as an intelligence clerk, "No one debriefed the pilots" after missions at Guadalcanal. He recalled that "a lot of us out there were civilians in uniform, and knew nothing of military recordkeeping. We did not keep mission reports at squadron level before the middle of 1943." Julius Jacobson confirmed, "I flew 111 missions in the South Pacific, and I was never debriefed even once." He didn't find this unusual after the Yamamoto mission because "it was not common practice."

Mitchell would come to deeply regret this informality.

I blame myself for not debriefing everybody, especially Lanphier, Barber, and Holmes. I should have known better because it was an important mission. We had good debriefings later in the war but we had no formal setup then. If I had done it myself right then and there, we wouldn't have this controversy today about who shot Yamamoto down. It would certainly have stopped a lot of the flak that Lanphier was throwing out that day and ever afterward.

About 25 to 40 officers and 50 to 100 enlisted men gathered, listening to the pilots give their accounts of the mission. Lanphier persisted in retelling his story over and over to anyone who would listen. Barber grew increasingly perturbed at this performance. Even if Lanphier's claim to a Betty was valid, how could he definitively assert it was the one carrying Yamamoto? Finally, he had had enough, and cut in: "How in the hell do you know you got Yamamoto?" Startled, Lanphier shot back, "You're a damn liar! You're a damn liar!" Barber was shocked at this reaction. "I hadn't made a statement. I just asked a question, but here he was calling me a damn liar for asking a question."

The other pilots of his graduating class (41-G) at Kelly Field, Texas, took five days' leave before reporting to the 35th Pursuit Group at Hamilton Field, but Doug Canning took ten and bought a new car so he could visit his family in Wayne, Nebraska. That meant he was left behind when his fellow graduates shipped out, and he was still in Fiji when their transport, the USS *Langley*, was sunk by Japanese aircraft south of Java on February 27, 1942. Among the hundreds of Americans KIA in this disaster were all 18 members of the 41-G graduating class. (Matt Simek)

Tom Lanphier, Besby Holmes, and Rex Barber look relatively convivial as they share the spotlight in the aftermath of the Yamamoto mission. To tamp down any contestation over claims and kill scores, all three had been credited with downing a Betty in the melee over Bougainville – a fiction that could not endure. With unintentional significance, the three men have been posed in front of P-38 No. 125 ("Diablo") – Barber's Lightning. (Matt Simek)

"There was absolutely no debriefing by anyone," Holmes claimed; because he was last to return, the other pilots had staked their claims in advance. "Naturally, I was mad as hell. The victories had been distributed before I could report what Ray [Hine] and I had done. And as a result, a few heated words were exchanged." Lanphier and Barber each received credit for one bomber, "but neither could confirm the other's claim," Holmes notes. In the immediate aftermath of the mission, "it was a toss-up as to who knocked down the Betty carrying Yamamoto. Which one was he in? We didn't know at that point."

Ruffled feathers were soothed when a compromise was arrived at whereby Lanphier, Barber, and Holmes would each take credit for downing a Betty. Later that day, the first of several classified operational messages, based on the informal reports of the personnel at Fighter Two, was prepared by Lieutenant Commander William A. Read, an administrative officer on Mitscher's staff who suggested that a good opening line was needed. The following top-secret dispatch (which garbled the commanding officer's name) was sent to Admiral Halsey:

POP GOES THE WEASEL
P-38S LED BY MAJOR [JOHN W.] MITCHELL USAAF VISITED KAHILI AREA
ABOUT 0930L SHOT DOWN TWO BOMBERS ESCORTED BY 6 ZEROS FLYING
CLOSE FORMATION
1 OTHER BOMBER SHOT DOWN BELIEVED ON TEST FLIGHT
3 ZEROS ADDED TO THE SCORE SUMS TOTAL 6

1 P-38 FAILED RETURN
APRIL 18 SEEMS TO BE OUR DAY

That final sentence was a reference to the launching of Jimmy Doolittle's B-25 bombers from the carrier *Hornet* against Japan on April 18 the year before. Mitscher had been in command of the *Hornet*, while Halsey had been in command of the 16-ship task force on the *Enterprise*.

An elated Halsey immediately replied:

CONGRATULATIONS TO YOU AND MAJOR MITCHELL AND HIS HUNTERS
SOUNDS AS THOUGH ONE OF THE DUCKS IN THEIR BAG WAS A PEACOCK.

Mitscher also instructed Read to prepare recommendations that all the survivors of the mission receive the Congressional Medal of Honor and spot promotion.

That evening, while the mission pilots drank and sang the night away at the Opium Den on Guadalcanal, the CINCPAC Command Summary noted: "It seems probable the CinC Combined was shot down in a plane over the Buin area today by Army P-38s." When the news was announced at Halsey's regular conference the next morning, Rear Admiral R. Kelly Turner whooped and applauded. Halsey cut him off; "Hold on, Kelly! What's so good about it? I'd hoped to lead that scoundrel up Pennsylvania Avenue in chains, with the rest of you kicking him where it would do the most good!"

An "official" Fighter Interception Report (FIR) was later drafted on Guadalcanal and forwarded to Halsey and Nimitz. It was signed by the intelligence officers who had helped Mitchell prepare the mission, Captain William Morrison and Lieutenant Joseph McGuigan. After describing the planning and the route flown to the interception point, the report continued:

When Lanphier and Barber were within one mile of contact, their attack was observed by the enemy. The bombers nosed down, one started a 360-degree turn dive, the other going out and away toward the shoreline; the Zeros dropped their belly tanks and three peeled down, in a string, to intercept Lanphier. When he saw that he could not reach the bomber he turned up and into the enemy, exploding the first Zero, and firing into the others as they passed. By this time he had reached 6,000 feet, so he nosed over, and went down to the treetops after his escaping objective. He came into the bomber broadside – and fired his bursts – a wing flew off and the plane went flaming to the earth.

The report described how Lanphier "hedgehopped the trees and made desperate maneuvers to escape" the escorting Zeros. "He kicked rudders, slipped, and skidded, tracers were flying past

Another perspective of Fighter Two. Note the crew tents in the foreground, and the complete absence of hangars or revetments to shelter or protect the aircraft parked to one side of the runway from either enemy action or the environment. (Matt Simek)

A Betty, trailing smoke from its burning right engine somewhere in the South Pacific. The American cover flight over Bougainville on April 18 could have witnessed the last moments of Yamamoto's Betty in the same configuration below them, Rex Barber's P-38 hanging doggedly on its tail. (Naval History and Heritage Command)

his plane, but he finally outran them." Meanwhile, Barber had tracked down the second bomber: "When he fired, the tail section flew off, the bomber turned over on its back and plummeted to earth."

According to the report, Holmes then noticed a third, "stray bomber near Moila Point flying low over the water. He dove on it, his bursts setting it smoking in the left engine; Hine also shot at it and Barber polished it off with a burst in the fuselage." Holmes, Hine, and Barber then turned for home; however, "Zeros were coming in on Barber's tail and Holmes whipped up and around and shot one down in flames." Barber also shot down a Zero, and it was "believed that Hine also accounted for a Zero as a total of three enemy fighters were seen to fall into the sea during this part of the combat."

The report appears to have distilled the accounts of the three survivors of the kill section, making the "official" score three Betty bombers and three Zeros shot down. "Not one dissent was expressed – from Mitchell, from Barber, from Lanphier, Viccellio" regarding this conclusion, Condon asserted: "Nothing." In reality, the claims dramatically inflated the number of enemy aircraft destroyed. There were only two Bettys over Bougainville that day, not three, and for all the talk of Zeros exploding or being shot down in flames, not one of them was lost during the engagement. In fact, not only did all six of the escort fighters survive, there was not a single bullet hole in any of them. After two hours at Ballale they were all given orders to return to Rabaul. Not that Japanese accounts were any more accurate. The combat record of the escort Zeros states: "Six enemy aircraft downed: Tsujinoue 2, Sugita 2, Hidaka and Yanagiya 1 each." The inherent tendency of fighter pilots in the heat of battle to embellish the action or exaggerate their achievements calls into question the veracity of any statement made. However, the report apparently placated the American pilots involved at the time, and any ill will over specific claims seems to have abated. Regarding individual scores in the aftermath of the mission, "I didn't give a damn," Mitchell said. "We did what we were supposed to do. It didn't make any difference to me who shot the Admiral down."

Indeed, the mood appears to have improved to the point where, a few days after the mission, having been granted ten days' R&R, Barber and Lanphier found themselves indulging in multiple rounds of golf together in Auckland,

New Zealand. At one point, Barber wondered out loud where the mission report had come from, given he, Mitchell, and Holmes were never consulted. According to Barber – who also asserts Brigadier-General Dean "Doc" Strother, the 13th Air Force FC Ops Officer who had joined them on the links, verified this conversation – Lanphier replied, "Don't worry about it, Rex. I went over to the Ops tent that evening and helped to draft the report and filled in the important details. I also helped write our citations for the Medal of Honor."

This would certainly be in character. Lanphier – a graduate of Stanford University with a bachelor's degree in Journalism – had apparently written several mission reports previously. His squadron mates would relate how he could always tell a good yarn, and how his stories always got better in the retelling.

Lanphier's zeal for the limelight would shortly backfire spectacularly. Senior AP war correspondent J. Norman Lodge later joined the golfing trio. On May 11, 1943, ten days before the Japanese formally admitted to the death of Yamamoto, US Navy censors on New Caledonia reviewed an article Lodge had submitted for approval which contained a detailed description of the top-secret mission and bluntly stated, "We have every reason to believe it was Yamamoto in one of the bombers." This potential breach of highly classified information was in direct contravention of an order explicitly laid down by Nimitz that "no publicity of any kind should be given this action." Barber and Lanphier were summoned to Halsey's office, where the Admiral tore into them without mercy. "He accused us of everything he could think of, from being traitors to our country to being so stupid we had no right to wear the American uniform," a chastened Rex Barber recalled. Halsey turned down the Medal of Honor recommendations he had received from Mitscher and informed the pilots, "as far as I'm concerned, none of you deserve even an Air Medal for what you did! You ought to face a court martial." Begrudgingly, Halsey did eventually approve their award of the Navy Cross. This action might have been nudged along by a guilty conscience, for Lodge had ended his article with the line, "Have every reason to believe one of your quail was a peacock and it was Yamamoto who was indeed that peacock," clearly derived from Halsey's own, unguarded, first response to Mitscher.

Lanphier would grasp one more opportunity to burnish his own image before the war was over. *Time* magazine had a correspondent on Guadalcanal, and Lanphier is known to have spoken with him. His interpretation of the mission heavily influenced the May 31 issue of the magazine, which featured a caricature of Yamamoto on its cover, and an article on page 28 reporting his death. The article ended with, "When the name of the man who killed Admiral Yamamoto is released, the U.S. will have a new hero." Readers did not have to wait long to uncover the mystery of who this might be. On page 66 of the same issue, an article entitled "Heroes, The Younger Generation" described a mission of 16 P-38 fighters flying near Kahili. While 12 fighters had climbed for top cover

The four near the water bored on, found unexpected game; three Jap bombers waddling home with a heavy cover of Zeros.

Mourners line the streets of Tokyo to pay their last respects as Yamamoto's funeral procession passes by, June 5, 1943. Yamamoto was only the twelfth commoner ever granted the honor of a state funeral. The mood in America was less somber. The president himself hugely enjoyed the occasion, drafting a mocking letter of condolence to Yamamoto's widow: "Time is a great leveler and somehow I never expected to see the old boy at the White House anyway. Sorry I can't attend the funeral because I approve of it. Hoping he is where we know he ain't. Very sincerely yours, Franklin Delano Roosevelt." (Getty Images)

The bombers lurched frantically for the cover of their own antiaircraft.

The Zeros piled into the Lightnings and both top covers swirled in a thundering dogfight. Down below, Lieutenant Rex T. Barber whipped into a bomber, sawed off its tail with a burst of fire, and knocked off a second as he pulled out of the attack.

The squadron commander, lean, black-eyed Captain Thomas G. Lanphier, tangled with a low-flying Zero, shot it down. He swung away, picked a bomber, shot it down, too. Up above the top cover fight had broken off. A mission had been completed. The squadron whisked back to the Solomons base, wondered if it nailed some Jap bigwig in the bombers.

Accompanying the article was a photo of a shirtless Lanphier, who was credited with being the squadron commander. No mention was made of Mitchell.

Confirmation of Yamamoto's fate could only come from the Japanese, and that was an agonizingly slow process. In the immediate aftermath of the operation, by land, sea, and air the Japanese desperately sought to reach the crash site, hoping against hope there might be survivors.

A detachment of the Seventeenth Army under Second Lieutenant Hamasuna, camped close to the native village of Aku, about 18 miles west of Buin, witnessed an aerial dogfight at an extremely low altitude above them early on the morning of April 18. Several hours later, Hamasuna received orders from regimental headquarters: "A plane carrying top navy brass has crashed. You are to organize a search party and go to look for it. You were watching, so you'll know roughly where it crashed."

Hamasuna selected a sergeant and nine other NCOs and men from his platoon. Two days later, they stumbled upon the wreckage of a Betty bomber. The wings and propellers had survived, but the fuselage had broken just in front of the Rising Sun insignia, and the section extending from there to the cockpit was a burned-out hulk. Significantly in light of Lanphier's later assertion the bomber's tail "was puffing a steady series of shots from the cannon lodged back there," no defensive armament was found or recovered in or around the downed aircraft.

There were no survivors. The bodies of the 11 crew and passengers were scattered about the wreckage. Among them was Yamamoto. He was still sitting upright in his seat, which had been thrown clear at impact. Still wearing his white gloves, his left hand grasped his sword, while his right hand rested lightly upon it. Yamamoto's watch had stopped at 0745hrs. According to an autopsy report, while sitting on the right-hand side of the Betty behind the copilot, facing forward, the Admiral had been killed by either of two .50cal machine-gun bullets. One had entered at the angle of his left lower jaw and emerged at the right eye, while the other had entered the center of the left shoulder blade, passing upward and to the right, with no exit wound.

An envelope was subsequently found in Yamamoto's safe aboard the *Musashi*: "Wait but a while, young men! One last battle, fought gallantly to the death, and I will be joining you!"

On May 7, the *Musashi* set sail from the Harushima anchorage at Truk carrying the ashes of Yamamoto and the others who had died with him. On May 21, it entered Tokyo Bay and dropped anchor off Kisarazu. On that day, Imperial Headquarters finally broke the news to the Japanese people. A Tokyo radio announcer interrupted the regular program to state: "In April this year, Admiral Yamamoto Isoroku, commander-in-chief of the Combined Fleet, met a gallant death on board his plane in an encounter with the enemy in the course of directing overall operations at the front line ..." The announcer broke down in tears and could not continue.

US codebreakers had long been aware of this fact prior to the official statement. Weeks earlier, imperial communication with the Combined Fleet had ceased being addressed to the C-in-C, being directed to his Chief of Staff instead. When the White House press corps asked the President what he thought of the formal announcement, the response was typically cryptic. "Is he dead?" Roosevelt asked, with a coy smile. "Gosh."

Yamamoto, who had been posthumously awarded the Grand Order of the Chrysanthemum, First Class, and the rank of Fleet Admiral, was accorded a state funeral on June 5, 1943 – the same day of the same month as the funeral of Admiral Togo Heihachiro nine years previously. That morning, his ashes were placed in a small coffin draped with a white cloth and placed on a black artillery caisson. The procession, led by a naval band playing Chopin's Funeral March, proceeded slowly to Hibiya Park near the Imperial Palace in the center of Tokyo. The roads were lined with mourners and an estimated three million Japanese crowded into the area near the cemetery to pay their last respects to a national hero. When the funeral was over, half of Yamamoto's ashes were interred in a grave next to that of Togo, while the other half was laid to rest at his home in Nagaoka.

Assessment

The Japanese selected Admiral Mineichi Koga as the new C-in-C of the Combined Fleet. Notified of his promotion, Koga responded, "There was only one Yamamoto and no one is able to replace him. His loss is an unsupportable blow to us." Koga was killed in an airplane crash in the Philippines on March 31, 1944. Admiral Soemu Toyoda and finally Admiral Jisaburo Ozawa succeeded him in turn at the head of the doomed and dying Imperial Japanese Navy.

The wreckage of Yamamoto's Betty still lies where it crashed on Bougainville. Long after the event, controversy still lingers about who, exactly, brought it down. The USAF asked historians in its Historical Division to verify the rival claims. After evaluating the limited primary documentation, the historians concluded Yamamoto's bomber had been fired on first by Barber and subsequently by Lanphier who watched it crash into the jungle a few moments later. Neither pilot had seen the actions of the other. Under rules applied by the Thirteenth Air Force at that time, if two or more pilots fired on an armed enemy aircraft in flight and destroyed it, they shared credit equally. Thus the credit was shared between the two men. Supporters of Lanphier's claim petitioned the USAF in 1985 for a reevaluation of the original finding. A board of air force historians was convened but, no new evidence having been submitted, the original award of a shared credit remained unaltered. (Jerry Hamlin, dinofish.com)

Given the ultimate outcome of the war, was the targeting of Yamamoto worth the risk of the Japanese realizing their communications were compromised and taking the appropriate steps in response? The British certainly thought not. Sir Stewart Graham Menzies, Chief of MI6, the British Secret Intelligence Service (SIS) during World War II, asserted the Yamamoto mission "demonstrated a predisposition in the command of the Southwest Pacific theater to use Magic for purely tactical or prestige purposes." Prime Minister Winston Churchill, in particular, thought the targeting of Yamamoto "was an act of self-indulgence, not a military operation." He demanded to know from Roosevelt how, exactly, the Allies gained from the death of Yamamoto. By killing him, the Americans removed from the scene a man whose strategies and tactics were well known to them, and the likelihood was that he would be replaced by one whose conduct of battles was unknown. But the overriding issue at stake was the sustainability of Magic. By committing to act on the intelligence breakthrough, the US accepted the risk that Magic "might be compromised at the very moment when, on a grander scale, it was being used to transform Japan from a first-rate marine power to a third-rate naval power whose operating radius was rapidly being confined to home waters."

Churchill pointed out that on numerous occasions the British could have staged the assassination of Erwin Rommel in much the same way as the Americans had of Yamamoto, but had elected not to do so because it might have led the Germans to tighten security around their Enigma codes, with disastrous consequences for the overall war effort. To that end, Churchill had even been prepared to sacrifice his own urban population. In November 1940, British codebreakers confirmed in advance the Luftwaffe was going to bomb the town of Coventry. Churchill decided it was better to keep silent and lose the town than to jeopardize Ultra. To show their displeasure, the British halted the exchange of Ultra- and Magic-related communications with the Americans for weeks after the Yamamoto mission, not resuming the interchange until later in May 1943.

In the immediate aftermath of the mission, the Japanese were certainly aware Yamamoto had been subjected to a premeditated interception. What struck Yanagiya was the clinical nature of the attack; that the Americans would materialize out of nowhere to strike "just one blow, and then just scatter to escape … Without confirmation, they just took off." There was no doubt in his mind the Americans knew who was inbound to Kahili. "It was deliberate. It was not an accident."

At the beginning the day after Yamamoto was shot down, the Guadalcanal-based P-38s made numerous sorties in the vicinity of Bougainville to give the impression the encounter on the 18th was simply coincidental. The Japanese were suspicious enough for Southeast Area Fleet command at Rabaul to send false coded messages saying that fleet commander Kusaka Jin'ichi was going to tour the front, but the Allies refused to take the bait and ignored these completely. The Japanese never identified the source of the Allied inside information on Yamamoto's itinerary and did not revamp their codes, enabling Magic to continue gleaning priceless intelligence from that source until the last days of the war. The main return on the mission from an American point of view was the boost in Allied morale; but given no leader subsequently emerged within the Japanese military who possessed a fraction of Yamamoto's tactical insight or domestic prestige, it's fair to say the mission was of concrete value in strategic terms. In that sense, the gamble was worth taking, and it paid off.

Legacies

Many of those who took part in the Yamamoto mission, on both sides, did not long survive the Admiral. Among the Americans, two top cover pilots were killed over the ensuing four and a half months. Gordon Whittaker was killed less than two weeks later on a mission over Bougainville, while Eldon Stratton was killed over Vella Tavella on the last day of August.

The Japanese fared worse. Of the six escorting Zero pilots, only one, Kenji Yanagiya, survived the war, in large part because he was badly wounded only two months after Yamamoto's death and invalided out of the

After the war, Major Rex Barber commanded the 29th FS, 412th FG, and later the 1st FG's 27th FS, flying Lockheed P-80s out of March Field, California. He is depicted here, second from right in the front row, June 12, 1946. Barber retired as a Colonel in April, 1961. (NARA)

service having lost one of his hands amputated. Four of the remaining pilots were killed within three months of the loss of Yamamoto. Two, Hidaka and Okazaki, were shot down and killed by American F4F fighters over the Russell Islands on 7 June. Another, Morizaki, was shot down and killed during a Japanese attack on Allied shipping near Guadalcanal on June 16. The fourth, Tsujinoue, flew escort for Japanese bombers attacking Rendova Island on July 1 and never returned. The fifth, Sugita, was shot down and killed over Japan in April 1945.

Conversely, others lived long and fruitful lives. After serving in both the European and Pacific theaters during World War II, and again in Korea, John W. Mitchell passed away in 1995. Besby Holmes died in 2006. Douglas Canning, the last survivor of the Yamamoto mission, died in 2016.

Having been promoted to Captain, after his tour of duty ended in June 1943, Rex Barber served in China as commander of the 449th Fighter Squadron, Fourteenth Air Force, flying 28 combat missions before being shot down in enemy territory; although seriously injured, he evaded capture thanks to the efforts of local civilians.

Barber continued to fly fighters after the war was over. He participated in initial test work with the Lockheed P-80 Shooting Star, the Air Force's first jet fighter, and commanded the first squadron in the Air Force to be equipped with jet fighter aircraft.

In 1950, Barber was sent to Korea on a special assignment during which he flew three combat missions. Subsequent posts included duty with the Air Defense Command and as air attaché in Colombia and Ecuador. He retired as a full Colonel in 1961 after 21 years of active duty. He died in July 2001.

Lanphier was assigned to the Pentagon. He was promoted to Major, was sent to Europe to survey fighter operations there, and made PR flights around the US. Promoted to Lieutenant Colonel in February 1945, he served as Director of Operations of the 72nd Fighter Wing of the Second Air Force. Leaving active duty following the war, he was promoted to Colonel in the Air Force Reserves in 1950. During that period, he worked as an editor of the *Idaho Statesman* and the *Boise Capital News*, and served as president of the Air Force Association. In 1949 he volunteered to fly around the world on commercial airlines to highlight the progress aviation had made in the 46 years since the Wright brothers' historic first flights at Kitty Hawk. Dramatically, Lanphier vowed he was going to break the record for round-the-world passenger travel of six days, three hours, and 40 minutes set in 1948 by Edward Eagan, chairman of the New York State Boxing Commission. Lanphier left New York on December 2, 1949, and returned in four days, 23 hours, 50 minutes. During his stopover in Tokyo, Lanphier claimed to have somehow made time to meet Yamamoto's widow.

Boosted by his connections and flair for self-publicity, Lanphier enjoyed a distinguished post-war career, becoming VP of Convair Aircraft Co., President of Fairbanks-Morse, a VP of Raytheon Corp., and a special assistant to Air Force Secretary Stuart Symington. His innate desire to command the limelight persisted to the end. In addition to "downing nine Japanese planes, damaging eight on the ground, and sinking a destroyer," the November 1987 obituary noting his burial in Arlington National Cemetery bluntly stated that "Lanphier shot down the plane carrying Admiral Isoroku Yamamoto."

Any controversy over the question of specific credit for the death of Yamamoto might have faded into the shadows of history had Lanphier not been so eager to go public with his account of the mission. Twice in 1944 he submitted narratives for security review, but it was not until after the war that his story was cleared and appeared in print in *The New York Times*. This inflamed old wounds among his erstwhile colleagues, none of whom was consulted beforehand.

"When this happened I couldn't have cared less who shot down Yamamoto. We got him and that was the whole thing," Mitchell commented. But many years later, he admitted Lanphier's subsequent claims for sole credit "have bothered me for a long time … I should have sounded off about it a long time ago."

The official "Transcript of Proceedings" by the Air Force Board for Correction of Military Records dated October 17–18, 1991, contains the testimony of Dr. Charles Darby, a New Zealand resident and geothermal engineer regarding his forensic investigations of the wreckage of Admiral Yamamoto's Betty bomber in 1972 and in 1988. His detailed analysis concluded the bomber, which was burning before it hit the ground, crashed through trees and impacted approximately 40 degrees nose down with both wings level. Power had been lost in both engines, and the propellers had either stopped or were windmilling very slowly. Darby testified the Betty had landed more or less intact, and "by no stretch of the imagination, could any large piece of the right wing have disappeared in flight." Furthermore, Darby testified all evidence of combat damage from bullets and chunks of molten airframe melted by impact from a shell were from the Barber attack position, "from immediately behind the bomber through the tail gunner's position and traveling forwards through the fuselage." In Darby's opinion, "There was no evidence on any remaining wreckage of an attack from the bomber's starboard beam as related in all of Lanphier's accounts."

Ross Channon, an Australian working for the Goodyear Rubber Company at Arawa, Bougainville, visited the wreckage site in 1985 and confirmed, "The right wing outer panel lay where that wing burned with the wreckage; apparently it did not detach in flight." Furthermore, "All visible gunfire and shrapnel damage was caused by bullets entering from

Major John W. Mitchell ended his tour at Guadalcanal with a personal score of eight kills. After a stint in Europe he returned to the Pacific theater, based in Iwo Jima with the 15th FG. Flying P-51 Mustangs escorting B-29 Superfortress bomber raids, he was credited with three more kills, ending the war with a total score of 11. Colonel Mitchell returned to active duty in June 1952, taking over the 51st Fighter-Interceptor Wing in South Korea. Flying the F-86 Sabre he shot down four MiG-15s. (Matt Simek)

The survivors of the mission pose for a group photo. Back row: 1st Lt. Roger Ames, 1st Lt. Lawrence Graebner, Capt. Thomas Lanphier, 1st Lt. Delton Goerke, 1st Lt. Julius Jacobson, 1st Lt. Eldon Stratton, 1st Lt. Albert Long, 1st Lt. Everett Anglin. Front row: 1st Lt. William Smith, 1st Lt. Douglas Canning, 1st Lt. Besby Holmes, 1st Lt. Rex Barber, Major John Mitchell, Major Louis Kittel, 2nd Lt. Gordon Whittaker. Absent are the MIA 1st Lt. Raymond Hine and – somewhat unfairly – 1st Lt. James McLanahan and 1st Lt. Joseph Moore, who were forced out of the flight by mechanical failure. Two of the pilots pictured – Whittaker and Stratton – would not survive the war. (Author's Collection)

immediately behind the bomber through the tail gunner's position, and traveling forwards through the fuselage."

Finally, the seat occupied by Admiral Yamamoto at the time of the attack and in which his dead body was found near the wreckage after the crash is preserved and on display in Japan today. The shrapnel damage to the rear of the seat matches the fatal back-wound described in the Yamamoto autopsy report.

The only partial corroboration of Lanphier's account comes from Hiroshi Hayashi, who has stated Yamamoto's Betty was attacked by two P-38s. The first attack was made from the right-hand side, while the second attack came from the left-hand side. Crucially, because it was only a matter of seconds after the second attack that the Betty crashed, he assumed the P-38 which made the attack from the left-hand side was responsible for shooting down Yamamoto's bomber, either because it killed or wounded the pilot or because it destroyed the Betty's control systems. He is convinced the aircraft attacking from the right-hand side missed Yamamoto's plane.

It is therefore just possible that Lanphier, while maneuvering to shake off the Zeros he had tangled with in the opening moments of the engagement, did encounter a Betty airborne at right angles to his flight path, i.e. heading south to his east. In the brief moment the bomber traversed his line of fire it is not impossible he was able to loose a few rounds in its general direction. His own account – which describes his angle as being "at about 70 degrees to the bomber, which is an impossible angle to hit anything" – suggests this. Beyond that, everything else in his narrative, which culminates in his fire tearing off the bomber's right wing and sending it plunging into the jungle, is pure fiction. Even while continuing to assert his own credit for the second bomber, 45 years after the event Holmes openly stated, "I have always thought that Barber shot the first Betty down."

The other pilots on the mission are also on record expressing deep skepticism about Lanphier's claims. "I could accept his judgment in making a head-on attack with the Zeros," Louis Kittel noted, "but I had then, and still have now, deep doubts on his ability to catch a diving Betty, much less make an almost 90-degree deflection shot from presumably out of range." Mitchell, too, was convinced that for Lanphier to have eliminated Yamamoto's bomber in the manner he described it, he would have had to have been the beneficiary of the most "improbable shot a pilot can make."

In fact, Mitchell has picked apart Lanphier's claim "the lead bomber made a 360-degree turn, first going back in the direction from which it had come, after it broke to the left." The other bomber was on the lead bomber's left, which would have meant the lead bomber crossed right in front of his wingman. An experienced pilot would not have risked such a maneuver, firstly because it "could have caused a midair collision," and secondly because turning away from the attacking P-38s was "inviting them to shoot his tail off. This doesn't make any sense."

Ultimately, Mitchell concluded, speaking for every other member of the flight regarding Lanphier's account of the action, "There is not a man here that saw anything like that … The fact is no one verified that Lanphier did this." In the final analysis, "there is no evidence, no confirmation by anyone, that Lanphier shot down a Zero fighter that day, that he shot down a bomber that day."

That leaves Barber, whose character, temperament and integrity have consistently commanded the utmost respect from his colleagues. His account emerges as the most viable, from the perspective of being both technically plausible and personally credible. "At no time ever do I recall anyone doubt what Barber said or what he did," Julius Jacobson, Mitchell's wingman, concluded. "The only thing ever questioned was what Lanphier said. I'm convinced that Barber mortally wounded that airplane and probably killed Yamamoto."

Perhaps the last word should go to the Japanese. In a sworn affidavit, Kenji Yanagiya, the only surviving Yamamoto mission Zero escort pilot and a man with no personal stake in ascribing its outcome to any individual American, stated:

> I saw one P-38 firing into the tail of Admiral Yamamoto's bomber and I saw the Admiral's airplane emitting smoke and flames while one P-38 was directly behind it. I saw the Admiral's airplane descend toward the jungle in an attitude of forced landing within 20 to 30 seconds from when I first saw one P-38 behind the Admiral's airplane firing into it. From the time that I first sighted any of the P-38s until the Admiral's airplane was down in the jungle was two minutes or less.

So far as Mitchell is concerned, Yanagiya's statement "is what I call a confirmation."

The irony is, Lanphier did not have to construct a false narrative of the events that morning in order to secure himself a place in history. His instinctive reaction to take on the escorting fighters at the moment of contact is what gave Barber the time and space in which to fulfill the mission. He played a critical role in a team effort that spanned the Pacific and incorporated personnel at all levels – from the cryptanalysts in their offices to the ground crews in their revetments to the pilots in their fighters. The dispute over credit should not be allowed to obscure the fact the operation was a triumph of intelligence, logistics, planning, and initiative. There can be few parallels in military history of a set-piece action being set up so perfectly and executed so brilliantly.

BIBLIOGRAPHY

Texts & Documentaries

Agawa, Hiroyuki, *The Reluctant Admiral*, Kodansha, New York, 1979

Davis, Burke, *Get Yamamoto*, Random House, New York, 1969

Davis, Don, *Lightning Strike: The Secret Mission to Kill Admiral Yamamoto and Avenge Pearl Harbor*, St. Martin's Press, New York, 2005

Glines, Carroll V., *Attack on Yamamoto*, Orion Books, New York, 1990

Hall, R. Cargill (ed.), *Lightning over Bougainville: The Yamamoto Mission Reconsidered*, Smithsonian Institution Press, Washington, DC, 1991

Hammel, Eric M., *Guadalcanal: Starvation Island*, Crown, New York, 1987

Hammel, Eric M., *Aces Against Japan*, Presidio, Novato, 1996

Hammel, Eric M., *Aces Against Japan II: The American Aces Speak*, Pacifica Military History, Pacifica, 2007

Hastings, Max, *The Secret War: Spies, Ciphers, and Guerillas, 1939–1945*, HarperCollins, New York, 2016

Hess, William N., *Pacific Sweep: The 5th and 13th Fighter Commands in World War II*, Kensington, New York, 1978

Holmes, Wilfred J., *Double-Edged Secrets: U.S. Naval Intelligence Operations in the Pacific during World War II*, Naval Institute Press, Annapolis, 1979

Hoyt, Edwin P., *Yamamoto: The Man Who Planned Pearl Harbor*, McGraw-Hill, New York, 1990

Hyder, Victor D., *Decapitation Operations: Criteria for Targeting Enemy Leadership*, US Army Command and General Staff College, Fort Leavenworth, 2004

Kagan, Neil and Hyslop, Stephen G., *The Secret History of World War II*, National Geographic, Washington, DC, 2016

Kahn, David, *The Codebreakers: The Comprehensive History of Secret Communication from Ancient Times to the Internet*, Scribner, New York, 1996

Layton, Edwin T., *And I Was There*, William Morrow and Co., New York, 1985

Prados, John, *Combined Fleet Decoded: The Secret History of American Intelligence and the Japanese Navy in World War II*, Naval Institute Press, Annapolis, 2001

Prados, John, *Islands of Destiny: The Solomons Campaign and the Eclipse of the Rising Sun*, NAL Caliber, New York, 2013

Simek, Matthew, *Attack on Yamamoto! The Daring Mission to Shoot Down Japan's Pacific Fleet Commander*, Pacific Vista Publishing, Newberg, 2008

Smith, Michael, *The Emperor's Codes: The Breaking of Japan's Secret Ciphers*, Arcade, New York, 2001

Stanaway, John, *P-38 Lightning Aces 1942–43*, Osprey, Oxford, 2014

Ugaki, Matome, *Fading Victory: The Diary of Admiral Matome Ugaki, 1941–1945*, University of Pittsburgh Press, Pittsburgh, 1991

Wolf, William, *13th Fighter Command in World War II: Air Combat over Guadalcanal and the Solomons*, Schiffer, Atglen, 2004

Articles

Amos, Bill, "Pacific Duty, Part III: Victory's Secrets," *The North Star Monthly*, January 1, 2011, http://www.northstarmonthly.com/features/pacific-duty---part-iii---victory-s/article_a9f8cc8e-bbcc-11e6-b850-df61ee4b87f6.html

Anonymous, "Use of outdated code led to ambush that killed Yamamoto, U.S. files show," *The Japan Times*, September 29, 2008, https://www.japantimes.co.jp/news/2008/09/29/national/use-of-outdated-code-led-to-ambush-that-killed-yamamoto-u-s-files-show/#.Xj7bfmj7RPY

Canning, Douglas S., "Who Shot Down Yamamoto?" *Air Force Magazine*, Vol. 89, No. 5, May 2006, pp. 7–8

Condon, John P., "Bringing Down Yamamoto," *US Naval Institute Proceedings*, Vol. 116, No. 11, November 1990, pp. 86–90

Haulman, Daniel L., "The Yamamoto Mission," *Air Power History*, Vol. 50, No. 2, Summer 2003, pp. 30–37

Hollway, Don, "Death by P-38," *Aviation History*, May 2013, http://www.historynet.com/death-by-p-38.htm

Huntington, Tom, "Who Shot Down Admiral Yamamoto?" *Air & Space Smithsonian*, Vol. 6, No. 6, February 1992, pp. 80–88

Pineau, Roger, "The Death of Admiral Yamamoto," *Naval Intelligence Professionals Quarterly*, Vol. 10, No. 4, October 1994, pp. 1–5

Taylor, Blaine, "Ambush in Hostile Skies," *Military History*, Vol. 5, No. 1, January 1988, pp. 42–49

INDEX